中国农业普查
CHINA AGRICULTURAL CENSUS
2016

Communique of the Third National Agricultural Census

第三次全国农业普查公报

国务院第三次全国农业普查领导小组办公室
中 华 人 民 共 和 国 国 家 统 计 局 著

The Steering Group Office of the Third National Agricultural Census of the State Council
National Bureau of Statistics of China

中国统计出版社
China Statistics Press

图书在版编目(CIP)数据

第三次全国农业普查公报 = Communique of the Third National Agricultural Census ：汉英对照 / 国务院第三次全国农业普查领导小组办公室，中华人民共和国国家统计局著. —— 北京 ：中国统计出版社，2018.5
ISBN 978—7—5037—8459—0

Ⅰ. ①第… Ⅱ. ①国… ②中… Ⅲ. ①农业—普查—统计资料—中国—汉、英 Ⅳ. ①F322—66

中国版本图书馆 CIP 数据核字(2018)第 072792 号

第三次全国农业普查公报
Communique of the Third National Agricultural Census

作　　者/国务院第三次全国农业普查领导小组办公室，中华人民共和国国家统计局
责任编辑/尹　伊
封面设计/黄俊杰
出版发行/中国统计出版社
通信地址/北京市丰台区西三环南路甲 6 号　邮政编码/100073
电　　话/邮购(010)63376909　书店(010)68783171
网　　址/http://www.zgtjcbs.com
印　　刷/北京厚诚则铭印刷科技有限公司
经　　销/新华书店
开　　本/880×1230mm　1/16
字　　数/90 千字
印　　张/4.75
版　　别/2018 年 5 月第 1 版
版　　次/2018 年 5 月第 1 次印刷
定　　价/78.00 元

目　录

Contents

第三次全国农业普查主要数据公报
(第一号)

国务院第三次全国农业普查领导小组办公室
中华人民共和国国家统计局
2017 年 12 月 14 日

为摸清“三农”基本国情,查清“三农”新发展新变化,国务院组织开展了第三次全国农业普查。这次普查的标准时点为 2016 年 12 月 31 日,时期资料为 2016 年度。普查对象包括农业经营户,居住在农村有确权(承包)土地或拥有农业生产资料的户,农业经营单位,村民委员会,乡镇人民政府。普查主要内容是农业生产能力及其产出、农村基础设施及其基本社会服务和农民生活条件等。农业普查采用全面调查的方法,由普查员对所有普查对象进行逐个查点和填报。全国共组织动员了普查员、普查指导员和各级普查机构的工作人员近 400 万人,登记了 2.3 亿农户、60 万个村级单位、4 万个乡级单位、200 多万个农业经营单位;组织 5 万多名工作人员对粮食、棉花等大宗农作物播种面积进行卫星遥感测量,完成了 10 多万景卫星遥感数据处理,实地调查了 11 万个样方和 2 万多个抽中普查区,实施了 2700 多架次整村无人机飞行测量,掌握了全国主要农作物种植空间分布,取得了全国各省(区、市)及种植大县主要农作物种植面积数据。

按照国际通行做法,国务院农普办组织了数据质量抽查,评估了普查数据质量。综合抽查结果显示,农业普查登记户的漏报率为 0.19%,普查指标数据差异率 0.40%。数据质量达到设计标准。

根据《全国农业普查条例》的有关规定,国务院农普办和国家统计局将分期发布普查公报,向社会公布普查的主要结果。

农业农村农民基本情况

第三次全国农业普查共调查了31925个乡镇，其中乡11081个，镇20844个；596450个村，其中556264个村委会，40186个涉农居委会；317万个自然村；15万个2006年以后新建的农村居民定居点。

一、农业经营主体

2016年，全国共有204万个农业经营单位。2016年末，在工商部门注册的农民合作社总数179万个，其中，农业普查登记的以农业生产经营或服务为主的农民合作社91万个；20743万农业经营户，其中，398万规模农业经营户。全国共有31422万农业生产经营人员。

二、农业机械拥有量

2016年末，全国共有拖拉机2690万台，耕整机513万台，旋耕机825万台，播种机652万台，水稻插秧机68万台，联合收获机114万台，机动脱粒机1031万台。

三、土地利用

2016年末，耕地面积[①]134921千公顷，实际经营的林地面积(不含未纳入生态公益林补偿面积的生态林防护林)203046千公顷，实际经营的牧草地(草场)面积224388千公顷。

四、农村基础设施

2016年末，在乡镇地域范围内，有火车站的乡镇占8.6%，有码头的占7.7%，有高速公路出入口的占21.5%；99.3%的村通公路。

2016年末，全国99.7%的村通电，11.9%的村通天然气。25.1%的村有电子商务配送站点。

2016年末，91.3%的乡镇集中或部分集中供水，90.8%的乡镇生活垃圾集中或部分集中处理。73.9%的村生活垃圾集中处理或部分集中处理，17.4%的村生活污水集中处理或部分集中处理，53.5%的村完成或部分完成改厕。

五、农村基本公共服务

2016年末，96.8%的乡镇有图书馆、文化站，11.9%的乡镇有剧场、影剧院，16.6%的乡镇有体育场馆，70.6%的乡镇有公园及休闲健身广场。59.2%的村有体育健身场所。

2016年末，96.5%的乡镇有幼儿园、托儿所，98.0%的乡镇有小学；32.3%的村有幼儿园、托儿所。

---

① 耕地面积使用国土资源部数据。

2016年末，99.9%的乡镇有医疗卫生机构，98.4%的乡镇有执业（助理）医师，66.8%的乡镇有社会福利收养性单位。81.9%的村有卫生室。

六、农民生活条件

2016年末，99.5%的户拥有自己的住房，47.7%的户使用经过净化处理的自来水，36.2%的户使用水冲式卫生厕所。

注：

1. 乡镇：指行政建制是乡、镇，包括重点镇、非重点镇和乡。不包括街道办事处和具有乡镇政府职能的农林牧渔场等管理机构。

2. 村：指村民委员会和涉农居民委员会所辖地域。

3. 自然村：指在农村地域内由居民自然聚居而形成的村落，自然村一般都应该有自己的名称。

4. 农业经营户：指居住在中华人民共和国境内（未普查港澳台），从事农、林、牧、渔业及农林牧渔服务业的农业经营户。

5. 规模农业经营户：规模农业经营户指具有较大农业经营规模，以商品化经营为主的农业经营户。规模化标准为：

种植业：一年一熟制地区露地种植农作物的土地达到100亩及以上、一年二熟及以上地区露地种植农作物的土地达到50亩及以上、设施农业的设施占地面积25亩及以上。

畜牧业：生猪年出栏200头及以上；肉牛年出栏20头及以上；奶牛存栏20头及以上；羊年出栏100只及以上；肉鸡、肉鸭年出栏10000只及以上；蛋鸡、蛋鸭存栏2000只及以上；鹅年出栏1000只及以上。

林业：经营林地面积达到500亩及以上。

渔业：淡水或海水养殖面积达到50亩及以上；长度24米的捕捞机动船1艘及以上；长度12米的捕捞机动船2艘及以上；其他方式的渔业经营收入30万元及以上。

农林牧渔服务业：对本户以外提供农林牧渔服务的经营性收入达到10万元及以上。

其他：上述任一条件达不到，但全年农林牧渔业各类农产品销售总额达到10万元及以上的农业经营户，如各类特色种植业、养殖业大户等。

6. 农业经营单位：指中华人民共和国境内（未普查港澳台）以从事农业生产经营活动为主的法人单位和未注册单位，以及不以农业生产经营活动为主的法人单位或未注册单位中的农业产业活动单位。既包括主营农业的农场、林场、养殖场、农林牧渔场、农林牧渔服务业单位、具有实际农业经营活动的农民合作社；也包括国家机关、社会团体、学校、科研单位、工矿企业、村民委员会、居民委员会、基金会等单位附属的农业产业活动单位。

7. 农业生产经营人员：指在农业经营户或农业经营单位中从事农业生产经营活动累计30天以上的人员数（包括兼业人员）。

8. 农民合作社：指有合作社的名称，符合《农民专业合作社法》中关于合作社性质、设立条件和程序、成员权利和义务、组织机构、财务管理等要求，有农业生产经营或农林牧渔服务，名称为农民合作社的农民互助性经济组织。包括已在工商部门登记，以及虽未登记但符合上述要求的农民合作社，不包括以公司名称登记注册的股份合作制企业、社区经济合作社、供销合作社、农村信用社等。也不包括从事农业生产资料购买、农产品加工、贮藏、运输、销售等非农行业的农民合作社。

9. 拖拉机：指发动机额定功率在2.2千瓦(含2.2千瓦)以上的拖拉机，包括小四轮与手扶式。

10. 耕整机：指自带发动机驱动，主要从事水田、旱田耕整作业的机械，包括微耕机、田园管理机等。

11. 旋耕机：指与拖拉机配套完成耕、耙作业的耕耘机械。

12. 播种机：包括条播机、穴播机、异型种子播种机、小粒种子播种机、根茎类种子播种机、撒播机、免耕播种机等。

13. 水稻插秧机：指自带动力驱动作业，用于水稻插秧的机械。

14. 联合收获机：指能一次完成作物收获的切割(摘穗)、脱粒、分离、清选等其中多项工序的机械。包括稻麦联合收割机、玉米联合收获机。

15. 机动脱粒机：指由动力机械驱动专门进行农作物脱粒的作业机械。

16. 实际经营的林地面积：指普查年度内，农业经营户和农业经营单位实际用于经营的林地面积。林地指生长乔木、竹类、灌木的土地，及沿海生长红树林的土地。包括迹地，不包括居民点内部的绿化林木用地，铁路、公路征地范围内的林木，以及河流、沟渠的护堤林。不包括未纳入生态公益林补偿面积的生态林防护林。

17. 实际经营的牧草地(草场)面积：指普查年度内，农业经营户和农业经营单位实际用于经营的牧草地(草场)面积。牧草地指以生长草本植物为主、用于畜牧业的土地。

18. 有火车站的乡镇：指在乡镇辖区内有国家铁道部门设立的能够正常进行货物或旅客运输的站点。

19. 有码头的乡镇：指在乡镇辖区内有在沿海、江、河、湖、水库等岸边建造的供船只停靠，主要用于货物或旅客运输的构筑物。不包括公园内的水域仅供游船停靠的码头。

20. 有高速公路出入口的乡镇：指在乡镇辖区内有符合中国交通部《公路工程技术标准》规定的高速公路出入口。

21. 有电子商务配送站点的村：指本村地域内有为网上购物等新型商品交易模式服务的配送站点。

22. 集中或部分集中供水的乡镇：指全部或部分住户通过城乡自来水管道网饮用自来水的乡镇。

23. 生活垃圾集中处理或部分集中处理的村：指本村地域内有垃圾处理设施进行垃圾集中处理，或者虽然没有垃圾处理设施，但是对垃圾实行统一集中清运处理。

24. 生活污水集中处理或部分集中处理的村：指本村地域内有污水处理设施进行污水集中处理，或者虽然没有污水处理设施，但是对污水实行统一集中收集由其他单位处理。

25. 完成或部分完成改厕的村：指本村地域内完成或部分完成了露天粪缸、粪坑、旱厕、简易厕所的改造，大多数或全部居民使用带有化粪池、沼气池或三隔池厕所，部分居民使用公共厕所或其他村里指定的定点场所作为倾倒粪便的场所。

26. 有图书馆、文化站的乡镇：指在乡镇辖区内有经过文化管理部门批准，并对公众开放的图书馆和文化站，不包括单位内部的图书室。

27. 有剧场、影剧院的乡镇：指乡镇辖区内有独立核算的专用剧场和属文化部门主管的能演出戏剧的影剧院、兼映电影的剧场，以及附属在剧院、团公开营业的非独立核算的剧场、排演场。

28. 有体育场馆的乡镇：指在乡镇辖区内有体育场和体育馆。体育场指有400米跑道(中心含足球场)，有固定道牙，跑道6条以上并有固定看台的室外田径场地。体育馆指有固定看台，可供篮球、排球、羽毛球、乒乓球、体操等项目训练比赛活动用的室内运动场地。包括学校或企事业单位的对外开放的各类体育场馆，但不包括体育健身广场。

29. 有公园及休闲健身广场的乡镇：指在乡镇辖区内有经过有关管理部门批准，供居民休闲游玩的地方。

30. 有体育健身场所的村：指本村地域内有由村集体、个人或其他机构举办的主要以服务公众为目的的、有固定场所和必要设施的体育活动站、馆、场所等。

31. 有幼儿园、托儿所的乡镇(村)：指乡镇(村)辖区内有幼儿园、托儿所，包括学前班，以及虽未经有关部门批准，但却有一定规模(儿童数超过10人)的个人办幼儿园、托儿所。

32. 有小学的乡镇：指乡镇辖区内有经过县及县以上教育部门批准，以招收适龄儿童为主实施小学教学计划的学校。

33. 有医疗卫生机构的乡镇：指在乡镇辖区内有从卫生行政部门取得《医疗机构执业许可证》、《计划生育技术服务许可证》，或从民政、工商行政、机构编制管理部门取得法人单位登记证书，为社会提供医疗保健、疾病控制、卫生监督服务或从事医学科研和医学在职培训等工作的单位。医疗卫生机构包括医院、基层医疗卫生机构、专业公共卫生机构、其他医疗卫生机构。

34. 有执业(助理)医师的乡镇：指在乡镇辖区内有1名或1名以上具有《医师执业证》及其“级别”为“执业医师”、“执业助理医师”且实际从事医疗、预防保健工作的人员，不包括有执业证但实际从事管理工作的医师。

35. 有社会福利收养性单位的乡镇：指在乡镇辖区内提供食宿、不以盈利为目的的伤残革命军人休养院、复退军人慢性病疗养院、复退军人精神病院、光荣院、社会福利院、儿童福利院、精神病福利院、老年收养性机构(敬老院、养老院、老年公寓)等收养性的社会福利事业单位的乡镇。

36. 有卫生室的村：指本村地域内，有经县及以上医疗主管部门许可，由各种经济组织和个人创办的卫生室(所、站)。卫生室(所、站)需要拥有固定经营场所，主要从事医疗卫生活动。不包括专业的牙医室，以及主要从事药品销售活动的单位。

37. 住房：一般指有墙、顶、门、窗等结构，周围有墙，能防风避雨，供人居住的房屋。按照各地生活习惯，可供居住的窑洞、竹楼、蒙古包、帐篷、毡房、船屋等也包括在内。

38. 经过净化处理的自来水：指通过自来水厂或集中净化设施进行净化和消毒、并符合国家饮用水标准的供人们生活的水。

39. 水冲式卫生厕所（冲入下水道、化粪池和厕坑）：指有上下水系统，或厕间有备水桶（瓢冲），坐便或蹲便器有水封或无水封的厕所，且粪便及污水冲入到下水道、化粪池和厕坑，无蝇，不会造成环境污染。

第三次全国农业普查主要数据公报
(第二号)

农业经营主体、农业机械和设施

国务院第三次全国农业普查领导小组办公室
中华人民共和国国家统计局
2017 年 12 月 15 日

第三次全国农业普查对全国农业经营主体、农业机械和设施进行了调查。现将主要结果公布如下：

一、农业经营主体数量

表 1　农业经营主体数量

单位：万户、万个

指　　标	全国	东部地区	中部地区	西部地区	东北地区
农业经营户	20743	6479	6427	6647	1190
＃规模农业经营户	398	119	86	110	83
农业经营单位	204	69	56	62	17
＃农民合作社	91	32	27	22	10

注：农民合作社指以农业生产经营或服务为主的农民合作社。

2016 年，全国农业经营户 20743 万户，其中规模农业经营户 398 万户。全国农业经营单位 204 万个。2016 年末，在工商部门注册的农民合作社总数 179 万个，其中，农业普查登记的以农业生产经营或服务为主的农民合作社 91 万个。

二、农业机械

2016 年末，全国拖拉机 2690 万台，耕整机 513 万台，旋耕机 825 万台，联合收获机 114 万台，播种机 652 万台，排灌动力机械 1431 万台。

表 2 主要农业机械数量

单位：万台、万套、万艘

指 标	全国	东部地区	中部地区	西部地区	东北地区
拖拉机	2690	758	888	582	463
耕整机	513	70	163	240	40
旋耕机	825	148	183	430	65
播种机	652	108	258	126	160
水稻插秧机	68	9	11	6	42
排灌动力机械	1431	442	521	384	84
联合收获机	114	33	45	16	20
机动脱粒机	1031	134	271	600	26
饲草料加工机械	409	23	37	303	46
挤奶机	10	2	1	5	2
剪毛机	5	1	1	2	0.5
增氧机	194	125	42	23	3
果树修剪机	49	21	13	14	0.6
内陆渔用机动船	28	13	10	3	1
海洋渔用机动船	25	22	0.0	1	2

三、农田水利设施

2016 年末，全国调查村中能够正常使用的机电井数量 659 万眼，排灌站数量 42 万个，能够使用的灌溉用水塘和水库数量 349 万个。

表 3 农田水利设施

单位：万眼、万个

指 标	全国	东部地区	中部地区	西部地区	东北地区
能正常使用的机电井数量	659	206	208	152	92
排灌站数量	42	18	16	7	1
能灌溉用的水塘和水库	349	43	224	78	4

2016 年末，全国灌溉耕地面积 61890 千公顷，其中有喷灌、滴灌、渗灌设施的耕地面积 10018 千公

顷;灌溉用水主要水源中,使用地下水的户和农业生产单位占30.5%,使用地表水的户和农业生产单位占69.5%。

表4 农田灌溉

单位:千公顷、%

指　　标	全国	东部地区	中部地区	西部地区	东北地区
灌溉耕地面积	61890	16044	20064	18633	7148
#有喷灌、滴灌、渗灌设施的耕地面积	10018	1655	1899	5079	1385
灌溉用水主要水源					
地下水	30.5	36.9	35.7	12.1	59.3
地表水	69.5	63.1	64.3	87.9	40.7

四、设施农业

2016年末,全国温室占地面积334千公顷,大棚占地面积981千公顷,渔业养殖用房面积7.6千公顷。

表5 设施农业

单位:千公顷

指　　标	全国	东部地区	中部地区	西部地区	东北地区
温室占地面积	334	130	41	95	69
大棚占地面积	981	474	186	215	106
渔业养殖用房面积	7.6	4.5	1.7	1.0	0.3

注:

1. 农业经营户:指居住在中华人民共和国境内(未普查港澳台),从事农、林、牧、渔业及农林牧渔服务业的农业经营户。

2. 规模农业经营户:规模农业经营户指具有较大农业经营规模,以商品化经营为主的农业经营户。规模化标准为:

种植业:一年一熟制地区露地种植农作物的土地达到100亩及以上、一年二熟及以上地区露地种植农作物的土地达到50亩及以上、设施农业的设施占地面积25亩及以上。

畜牧业:生猪年出栏200头及以上;肉牛年出栏20头及以上;奶牛存栏20头及以上;羊年出栏100只及以上;肉鸡、肉鸭年出栏10000只及以上;蛋鸡、蛋鸭存栏2000只及以上;鹅年出栏1000只及以上。

林业:经营林地面积达到500亩及以上。

渔业:淡水或海水养殖面积达到50亩及以上;长度24米的捕捞机动船1艘及以上;长度12米的捕捞机动船2艘及以上;其他方式的渔业经营收入30万元及以上。

农林牧渔服务业:对本户以外提供农林牧渔服务的经营性收入达到10万元及以上。

其他：上述任一条件达不到，但全年农林牧渔业各类农产品销售总额达到10万元及以上的农业经营户，如各类特色种植业、养殖业大户等。

3. 农业经营单位：指中华人民共和国境内（未普查港澳台）以从事农业生产经营活动为主的法人单位和未注册单位，以及不以农业生产经营活动为主的法人单位或未注册单位中的农业产业活动单位。既包括主营农业的农场、林场、养殖场、农林牧渔场、农林牧渔服务业单位、具有实际农业经营活动的农民合作社；也包括国家机关、社会团体、学校、科研单位、工矿企业、村民委员会、居民委员会、基金会等单位附属的农业产业活动单位。

4. 农民合作社：指有合作社的名称，符合《农民专业合作社法》中关于合作社性质、设立条件和程序、成员权利和义务、组织机构、财务管理等要求，有农业生产经营或农林牧渔服务，名称为农民合作社的农民互助性经济组织。包括已在工商部门登记，以及虽未登记但符合上述要求的农民合作社，不包括以公司名称登记注册的股份合作制企业、社区经济合作社、供销合作社、农村信用社等。也不包括从事农业生产资料购买、农产品加工、贮藏、运输、销售等非农行业的农民合作社。

5. 拖拉机：指发动机额定功率在2.2千瓦（含2.2千瓦）以上的拖拉机，包括小四轮与手扶式。

6. 耕整机：指自带发动机驱动，主要从事水田、旱田耕整作业的机械，包括微耕机、田园管理机等。

7. 旋耕机：指与拖拉机配套完成耕、耙作业的耕耘机械。

8. 播种机：包括条播机、穴播机、异型种子播种机、小粒种子播种机、根茎类种子播种机、撒播机、免耕播种机等。

9. 水稻插秧机：指自带动力驱动作业，用于水稻插秧的机械。

10. 联合收获机：指能一次完成作物收获的切割（摘穗）、脱粒、分离、清选等其中多项工序的机械。包括稻麦联合收割机、玉米联合收获机。

11. 机动脱粒机：指由动力机械驱动专门进行农作物脱粒的作业机械。

12. 灌溉耕地面积：指实际耕种的耕地中，有灌溉设施、有水源，正常气候下能灌溉的耕地面积。

13. 温室、大棚占地面积：由三部分组成，一是实际使用面积，指沿墙内侧的围绕面积；二是墙体面积，指设施的墙体等其他支撑体自身的占地面积；三是采光占用面积，指设施距遮光物体（其他设施、房屋等）的必要距离所占的面积。

14. 四大地区：东部地区包括北京市、天津市、河北省、上海市、江苏省、浙江省、福建省、山东省、广东省、海南省。中部地区包括山西省、安徽省、江西省、河南省、湖北省、湖南省。西部地区包括内蒙古自治区、广西壮族自治区、重庆市、四川省、贵州省、云南省、西藏自治区、陕西省、甘肃省、青海省、宁夏回族自治区、新疆维吾尔自治区。东北地区包括辽宁省、吉林省、黑龙江省。

15. 部分数据因四舍五入的原因，存在着与分项合计不等的情况。

第三次全国农业普查主要数据公报
(第三号)

农村基础设施建设和基本社会服务

国务院第三次全国农业普查领导小组办公室
中华人民共和国国家统计局
2017年12月15日

第三次全国农业普查对全国31925个乡镇和596450个村的基础设施建设和基本社会服务进行了调查,现将主要结果公布如下:

一、交通

2016年末,在乡镇地域范围内有火车站的乡镇占全部乡镇的8.6%,有码头的占7.7%,有高速公路出入口的占21.5%。

99.3%的村通公路,61.9%的村内主要道路有路灯。村委会到最远自然村、居民定居点距离以5公里以内为主。

表 1 乡镇、村交通设施

单位：%

指 标	全国	东部地区	中部地区	西部地区	东北地区
有火车站的乡镇	8.6	7.6	8.3	7.7	18.0
有码头的乡镇	7.7	10.0	8.5	6.7	3.3
有高速公路出入口的乡镇	21.5	28.9	22.6	17.0	19.9
通公路的村	99.3	99.9	99.5	98.3	99.7
按通村主要道路路面类型分的村					
#水泥路面	76.4	76.4	86.1	70.2	59.3
柏油路面	20.2	22.2	12.3	22.5	35.1
沙石路面	2.3	0.6	1.0	5.3	3.5
按村内主要道路路面类型分的村					
#水泥路面	80.9	84.0	89.7	72.7	60.0
柏油路面	8.6	11.1	3.4	9.0	15.9
沙石路面	6.7	2.4	4.7	11.7	18.9
村内主要道路有路灯的村	61.9	85.9	59.8	35.5	54.1
村委会到最远自然村或居民定居点距离					
5 公里以内	90.8	97.1	93.0	80.7	90.9
6—10 公里	6.6	2.3	5.5	13.0	7.1
11—20 公里	2.0	0.5	1.3	4.6	1.6
20 公里以上	0.6	0.1	0.2	1.7	0.4

二、能源、通讯

2016 年末，99.7%的村通电，11.9%的村通天然气，99.5%的村通电话，82.8%的村安装了有线电视，89.9%的村通宽带互联网，25.1%的村有电子商务配送站点。

表 2 村能源、通讯设施

单位：%

指 标	全国	东部地区	中部地区	西部地区	东北地区
通电的村	99.7	100.0	99.9	99.2	100.0
通天然气的村	11.9	10.3	8.4	18.3	4.7
通电话的村	99.5	100.0	99.7	98.7	100.0
安装了有线电视的村	82.8	94.7	82.9	65.5	95.7
通宽带互联网的村	89.9	97.1	92.7	77.3	96.5
有电子商务配送站点的村	25.1	29.4	22.9	21.9	24.1

三、环境卫生

2016 年末，91.3%的乡镇集中或部分集中供水，90.8%的乡镇生活垃圾集中处理或部分集中处理。

73.9%的村生活垃圾集中处理或部分集中处理,17.4%的村生活污水集中处理或部分集中处理,53.5%的村完成或部分完成改厕。

表3 乡镇、村卫生处理设施

单位:%

指 标	全国	东部地区	中部地区	西部地区	东北地区
集中或部分集中供水的乡镇	91.3	96.1	93.1	87.1	93.6
生活垃圾集中处理或部分集中处理的乡镇	90.8	94.6	92.8	89.0	82.3
生活垃圾集中处理或部分集中处理的村	73.9	90.9	69.7	60.3	53.1
生活污水集中处理或部分集中处理的村	17.4	27.1	12.5	11.6	7.8
完成或部分完成改厕的村	53.5	64.5	49.1	49.1	23.7

四、文化教育

2016年末,96.5%的乡镇有幼儿园、托儿所,98.0%的乡镇有小学,96.8%的乡镇有图书馆、文化站,11.9%的乡镇有剧场、影剧院,16.6%的乡镇有体育场馆,70.6%的乡镇有公园及休闲健身广场。

32.3%的村有幼儿园、托儿所,59.2%的村有体育健身场所,41.3%的村有农民业余文化组织。

表4 乡镇、村文化教育设施

单位:%

指 标	全国	东部地区	中部地区	西部地区	东北地区
有幼儿园、托儿所的乡镇	96.5	98.7	98.3	94.0	96.9
有小学的乡镇	98.0	98.7	99.5	97.3	95.2
有图书馆、文化站的乡镇	96.8	96.2	98.0	96.6	95.2
有剧场、影剧院的乡镇	11.9	18.5	14.4	7.9	5.9
有体育场馆的乡镇	16.6	20.5	19.4	13.5	12.1
有公园及休闲健身广场的乡镇	70.6	83.2	73.9	59.4	84.0
有幼儿园、托儿所的村	32.3	29.6	36.5	33.0	25.8
有体育健身场所的村	59.2	72.2	55.5	46.0	62.8
有农民业余文化组织的村	41.3	44.4	40.8	36.7	47.1

五、医疗和社会福利机构

2016年末,99.9%的乡镇有医疗卫生机构,98.4%的乡镇有执业(助理)医师,66.8%的乡镇有社会福利收养性单位,56.4%的乡镇有本级政府创办的敬老院。

81.9%的村有卫生室,54.9%的村有执业(助理)医师。

表 5 乡镇、村医疗和社会福利机构

单位：%

指　　标	全国	东部地区	中部地区	西部地区	东北地区
有医疗卫生机构的乡镇	99.9	99.9	100.0	99.8	99.7
有执业(助理)医师的乡镇	98.4	99.6	99.8	96.7	99.3
有社会福利收养性单位的乡镇	66.8	71.7	87.7	53.3	57.0
有本级政府创办的敬老院的乡镇	56.4	61.9	78.0	43.3	40.8
有卫生室的村	81.9	71.9	89.3	86.9	86.2
有执业(助理)医师的村	54.9	49.4	66.7	49.9	60.6

六、市场建设

2016 年末，68.1%的乡镇有商品交易市场，39.4%的乡镇有以粮油、蔬菜、水果为主的专业市场，10.8%的乡镇有以畜禽为主的专业市场，4.3%的乡镇有以水产为主的专业市场。

47.5%的村有 50 平方米以上的综合商店或超市，4.9%的村开展旅游接待服务，30.0%的村有营业执照的餐馆。

表 6 乡镇、村市场

单位：%

指　　标	全国	东部地区	中部地区	西部地区	东北地区
有商品交易市场的乡镇	68.1	75.5	72.3	62.0	65.1
有以粮油、蔬菜、水果为主的专业市场的乡镇	39.4	40.2	43.8	36.2	40.7
有以畜禽为主的专业市场的乡镇	10.8	7.7	12.9	12.2	5.0
有以水产为主的专业市场的乡镇	4.3	5.3	7.2	2.5	1.7
有 50 平方米以上的综合商店或超市的村	47.5	50.2	54.8	34.0	65.6
开展旅游接待服务的村	4.9	3.8	4.6	6.9	3.2
有营业执照的餐馆的村	30.0	31.3	32.4	26.6	27.1

注：

1. 乡镇：指行政建制是乡、镇，包括重点镇、非重点镇和乡。不包括街道办事处和具有乡镇政府职能的农林牧渔场等管理机构。

2. 村：指村民委员会和涉农居民委员会所辖地域。

3. 村内主要道路有路灯的村：指本村地域内的主要道路由村集体或其他单位统一组织安装了路灯。道路两旁由住户零星安装在门前的灯不包括在内。

4. 有电子商务配送站点的村：指本村地域内有为网上购物等新型商品交易模式服务的配送站点。

5. 集中或部分集中供水的乡镇：指全部或部分住户通过城乡自来水管道网饮用自来水的乡镇。

6. 生活垃圾集中处理或部分集中处理的村：指本村地域内有垃圾处理设施进行垃圾集中处理，或者虽然没有垃圾处理设施,但是对垃圾实行统一集中清运处理。

7. 完成或部分完成改厕的村:指本村地域内完成或部分完成了露天粪缸、粪坑、旱厕、简易厕所的改造,大多数或全部居民使用带有化粪池、沼气池或三隔池厕所,部分居民使用公共厕所或其他村里指定的定点场所作为倾倒粪便的场所。

8. 有社会福利收养性单位的乡镇:指在乡镇辖区内提供食宿、不以盈利为目的的伤残革命军人休养院、复退军人慢性病疗养院、复退军人精神病院、光荣院、社会福利院、儿童福利院、精神病福利院、老年收养性机构(敬老院、养老院、老年公寓)等收养性的社会福利事业单位的乡镇。

9. 有卫生室的村:指在本村地域内,经县及以上医疗主管部门许可,由各种经济组织和个人创办的卫生室(所、站)。卫生室(所、站)需要拥有固定经营场所,主要从事医疗卫生活动。不包括专业的牙医室,以及主要从事药品销售活动的单位。

10. 开展旅游接待服务的村:指有营业执照,在本村地域内从事旅游接待、餐饮和住宿等服务的居民户。包括提供茶馆、酒馆、乡村旅店、农家乐等活动的居民户。

11. 有商品交易市场的乡镇:指在乡镇辖区内经有关部门和组织批准设立,有固定场所、设施,有经营管理部门和监管人员,若干市场经营者入内,常年或实际开业三个月以上,集中、公开、独立地进行生活消费品、生产资料等现货商品交易以及提供相关服务的交易场所,包括各类消费品市场、生产资料市场等的乡镇。

12. 四大地区:东部地区包括北京市、天津市、河北省、上海市、江苏省、浙江省、福建省、山东省、广东省、海南省。中部地区包括山西省、安徽省、江西省、河南省、湖北省、湖南省。西部地区包括内蒙古自治区、广西壮族自治区、重庆市、四川省、贵州省、云南省、西藏自治区、陕西省、甘肃省、青海省、宁夏回族自治区、新疆维吾尔自治区。东北地区包括辽宁省、吉林省、黑龙江省。

13. 部分数据因四舍五入的原因,存在着与分项合计不等的情况。

第三次全国农业普查主要数据公报
（第四号）

农村生活条件

国务院第三次全国农业普查领导小组办公室
中华人民共和国国家统计局
2017 年 12 月 16 日

第三次全国农业普查对 23027 万农户的生活条件进行了调查。现将主要结果公布如下：

一、住房

2016 年末，99.5％的农户拥有自己的住房。其中，拥有 1 处住房的 20030 万户，占 87.0％；拥有 2 处住房的 2677 万户，占 11.6％；拥有 3 处及以上住房的 196 万户，占 0.9％；拥有商品房的 1997 万户，占 8.7％。

农户住房主要为砖混和砖（石）木结构。住房为砖混结构的 13182 万户，占 57.2％；砖（石）木结构的 5993 万户，占 26.0％；钢筋混凝土结构的 2884 万户，占 12.5％；竹草土坯结构的 640 万户，占 2.8％；其他结构的 329 万户，占 1.4％。

表 1 住房数量与结构构成

单位:%、万户

指　　标	全国	东部地区	中部地区	西部地区	东北地区
按拥有住房数量划分构成					
拥有 1 处住房	87.0	82.7	87.9	89.5	93.9
拥有 2 处住房	11.6	15.6	11.0	9.2	5.0
拥有 3 处及以上住房	0.9	1.4	0.7	0.5	0.3
没有住房	0.5	0.3	0.4	0.9	0.8
按住房结构划分构成					
钢筋混凝土	12.5	15.7	13.5	9.5	5.3
砖混	57.2	57.9	65.3	50.6	47.8
砖(石)木	26.0	25.1	18.9	30.9	42.5
竹草土坯	2.8	0.9	1.5	5.9	3.6
其他	1.4	0.5	0.8	3.1	0.9
拥有商品房户数	1997	767	557	577	96
拥有商品房农户所占比重	8.7	10.1	8.1	8.0	7.4

二、饮用水

10995 万户的饮用水为经过净化处理的自来水，占 47.7%;9572 万户的饮用水为受保护的井水和泉水，占 41.6%;2011 万户的饮用水为不受保护的井水和泉水，占 8.7%;130 万户的饮用水为江河湖泊水，占 0.6%;155 万户的饮用水为收集雨水，占 0.7%;67 万户的饮用水为桶装水，占 0.3%;96 万户饮用其他水源，占 0.4%。

表 2 按饮用水来源划分的住户构成

单位:%

指　　标	全国	东部地区	中部地区	西部地区	东北地区
经过净化处理的自来水	47.7	62.3	43.9	38.2	36.1
受保护的井水和泉水	41.6	33.5	42.8	45.8	58.5
不受保护的井水和泉水	8.7	3.5	11.9	11.8	5.3
江河湖泊水	0.6	0.1	0.4	1.3	0.0
收集雨水	0.7	0.0	0.4	1.7	0.0
桶装水	0.3	0.2	0.4	0.4	0.0
其他水源	0.4	0.3	0.3	0.8	0.1

三、卫生设施

使用水冲式卫生厕所的 8339 万户，占 36.2%;使用水冲式非卫生厕所的 721 万户，占 3.1%;使用卫生旱厕的 2859 万户，占 12.4%;使用普通旱厕的 10639 万户，占 46.2%;无厕所的 469 万户，占2.0%。

表3 按家庭卫生设施类型分的住户构成

单位：%

指　　标	全国	东部地区	中部地区	西部地区	东北地区
水冲式卫生厕所	36.2	54.2	29.2	29.7	4.1
水冲式非卫生厕所	3.1	2.1	4.1	3.8	0.2
卫生旱厕	12.4	11.7	13.6	12.0	12.2
普通旱厕	46.2	30.8	52.2	50.1	82.9
无厕所	2.0	1.2	0.9	4.3	0.5

四、拥有耐用消费品情况

平均每百户拥有小汽车24.8辆，摩托车、电瓶车101.9辆，淋浴热水器57.2台，空调52.8台，电冰箱85.9台，彩色电视机115.2台，电脑32.2台，手机244.3部。

表4 主要耐用消费品拥有量

指　　标	单位	全国	东部地区	中部地区	西部地区	东北地区
小汽车	辆/百户	24.8	33.7	22.4	18.8	17.6
摩托车、电瓶车	辆/百户	101.9	131.9	106.6	72.9	63.0
淋浴热水器	台/百户	57.2	77.2	59.4	42.5	10.3
空调	台/百户	52.8	86.8	58.5	20.5	2.2
电冰箱	台/百户	85.9	94.9	87.1	75.1	86.2
彩色电视机	台/百户	115.2	128.6	115.3	102.6	106.6
按电视节目接收方式分的户比重						
#有线电视接收	%	57.3	76.1	53.1	36.2	83.2
卫星接收	%	40.5	20.5	44.8	62.7	15.1
电脑	台/百户	32.2	50.3	31.1	15.9	23.5
手机	部/百户	244.3	247.9	247.4	243.1	214.0
上过互联网手机比重	%	47.8	48.8	47.4	47.4	46.2

注：按电视节目接收方式分的户比重是指使用不同电视节目接收方式的户占拥有彩色电视机户数的比重；上过互联网手机比重是指上过互联网手机数量占登记户拥有手机总数的比重。

五、主要生活能源

农民做饭取暖使用的能源中，主要使用电的13503万户，占58.6%；主要使用煤气、天然气、液化石油气的11347万户，占49.3%；主要使用柴草的10177万户，占44.2%；主要使用煤的5506万户，占23.9%；主要使用沼气的156万户，占0.7%；使用其他能源的126万户，占0.5%；主要使用太阳能的56万户，占0.2% 。

表 5 主要生活能源构成

单位:%

指 标	全国	东部地区	中部地区	西部地区	东北地区
柴草	44.2	27.4	40.1	58.6	84.5
煤	23.9	29.4	16.3	24.8	27.4
煤气、天然气、液化石油气	49.3	69.5	58.2	24.5	20.3
沼气	0.7	0.3	0.7	1.2	0.1
电	58.6	57.2	59.3	59.5	58.7
太阳能	0.2	0.2	0.3	0.3	0.1
其他	0.5	0.2	0.2	1.3	0.1

注:此指标每户可选两项,分项之和大于100%。

注:

1. 住房:一般指有墙、顶、门、窗等结构,周围有墙,能防风避雨,供人居住的房屋。按照各地生活习惯,可供居住的窑洞、竹楼、蒙古包、帐篷、毡房、船屋等也包括在内。

2. 做饭、取暖用能源:指住户在家庭炊事和取暖中使用的主要能源,包括柴草、煤、煤气、天然气、液化石油气、沼气、电、太阳能,以及其他能源如牛粪等。

3. 四大地区:东部地区包括北京市、天津市、河北省、上海市、江苏省、浙江省、福建省、山东省、广东省、海南省。中部地区包括山西省、安徽省、江西省、河南省、湖北省、湖南省。西部地区包括内蒙古自治区、广西壮族自治区、重庆市、四川省、贵州省、云南省、西藏自治区、陕西省、甘肃省、青海省、宁夏回族自治区、新疆维吾尔自治区。东北地区包括辽宁省、吉林省、黑龙江省。

4. 部分数据因四舍五入的原因,存在着与分项合计不等的情况。

第三次全国农业普查主要数据公报
（第五号）

农业生产经营人员情况

国务院第三次全国农业普查领导小组办公室
中华人民共和国国家统计局
2017 年 12 月 16 日

第三次全国农业普查对全国农业生产经营人员情况进行了调查。现将主要结果公布如下：

一、农业生产经营人员数量和结构

2016 年，全国农业生产经营人员 31422 万人，其中女性 14927 万人。在农业生产经营人员中，年龄 35 岁及以下的 6023 万人，年龄在 36 至 54 岁之间的 14848 万人，年龄 55 岁及以上的 10551 万人。

表 1 农业生产经营人员数量和结构

单位：万人、%

指　　标	全国	东部地区	中部地区	西部地区	东北地区
农业生产经营人员总数	31422	8746	9809	10734	2133
农业生产经营人员性别构成					
男性	52.5	52.4	52.6	52.1	54.3
女性	47.5	47.6	47.4	47.9	45.7
农业生产经营人员年龄构成					

续表

单位:万人、%

指　　标	全国	东部地区	中部地区	西部地区	东北地区
年龄 35 岁及以下	19.2	17.6	18.0	21.9	17.6
年龄 36—54 岁	47.3	44.5	47.7	48.6	49.8
年龄 55 岁及以上	33.6	37.9	34.4	29.5	32.6
农业生产经营人员受教育程度构成					
未上过学	6.4	5.3	5.7	8.7	1.9
小学	37.0	32.5	32.7	44.7	36.1
初中	48.4	52.5	52.6	39.9	55.0
高中或中专	7.1	8.5	7.9	5.4	5.6
大专及以上	1.2	1.2	1.1	1.2	1.4
农业生产经营人员主要从事农业行业构成					
种植业	92.9	93.3	94.4	91.8	90.1
林业	2.2	2.0	1.8	2.8	2.0
畜牧业	3.5	2.4	2.6	4.6	6.4
渔业	0.8	1.6	0.6	0.3	0.5
农林牧渔服务业	0.6	0.7	0.6	0.5	1.0

二、规模农业经营户农业生产经营人员数量和结构

2016 年,规模农业经营户农业生产经营人员(包括本户生产经营人员及雇佣人员)1289 万人,其中女性 609 万人,年龄 35 岁及以下的 272 万人,年龄在 36 至 54 岁之间的 751 万人,年龄 55 岁及以上的 266 万人。

表 2　规模农业经营户农业生产经营人员数量和结构

单位:万人、%

指　　标	全国	东部地区	中部地区	西部地区	东北地区
农业生产经营人员总数	1289	382	280	411	217
农业生产经营人员性别构成					
男性	52.8	54.0	53.7	50.0	54.7
女性	47.2	46.0	46.3	50.0	45.3
农业生产经营人员年龄构成					
年龄 35 岁及以下	21.1	16.8	17.1	27.0	22.6
年龄 36—54 岁	58.3	57.8	58.7	57.9	59.2
年龄 55 岁及以上	20.7	25.4	24.3	15.1	18.2
农业生产经营人员受教育程度构成					
未上过学	3.6	3.4	3.7	5.2	1.0
小学	30.6	28.8	26.9	35.7	28.6
初中	55.4	56.5	56.8	48.6	64.3

续表

单位:万人、%

指　　标	全国	东部地区	中部地区	西部地区	东北地区
高中或中专	8.9	9.9	11.2	8.4	5.2
大专及以上	1.5	1.3	1.4	2.1	0.9
农业生产经营人员主要从事农业行业构成					
种植业	67.7	60.0	60.9	73.3	79.8
林业	2.7	2.9	3.0	3.1	1.1
畜牧业	21.3	19.3	28.6	21.6	14.6
渔业	6.4	15.5	4.6	1.0	2.8
农林牧渔服务业	1.9	2.3	2.9	1.1	1.6

三、农业经营单位农业生产经营人员数量和结构

2016 年,农业经营单位农业生产经营人员 1092 万人,其中女性 444 万人,年龄 35 岁及以下的 215 万人,年龄在 36 至 54 岁之间的 668 万人,年龄 55 岁及以上的 209 万人。

表 3　农业经营单位农业生产经营人员数量和结构

单位:万人、%

指　　标	全国	东部地区	中部地区	西部地区	东北地区
农业生产经营人员总数	1092	341	265	358	128
农业生产经营人员性别构成					
男性	59.4	59.1	60.1	56.7	66.1
女性	40.6	40.9	39.9	43.3	33.9
农业生产经营人员年龄构成					
年龄 35 岁及以下	19.7	17.0	17.1	23.1	22.9
年龄 36—54 岁	61.2	59.7	61.2	61.7	63.6
年龄 55 岁及以上	19.1	23.3	21.7	15.3	13.5
农业生产经营人员受教育程度构成					
未上过学	3.5	3.4	3.5	4.6	1.2
小学	21.8	23.4	20.6	25.6	9.8
初中	47.0	48.6	49.7	44.3	44.5
高中或中专	19.6	17.9	20.1	16.7	31.3
大专及以上	8.0	6.7	6.1	8.9	13.2
农业生产经营人员主要从事农业行业构成					
种植业	50.3	49.6	49.1	50.7	53.3
林业	16.4	14.9	14.9	16.7	22.6
畜牧业	16.6	14.7	18.7	18.6	11.8
渔业	6.2	10.5	5.8	3.4	2.9
农林牧渔服务业	10.6	10.4	11.5	10.6	9.5

注:

1. 农业生产经营人员:指在农业经营户或农业经营单位中从事农业生产经营活动累计 30 天以上的人员数(包括兼业人员)。

2. 四大地区:东部地区包括北京市、天津市、河北省、上海市、江苏省、浙江省、福建省、山东省、广东省、海南省。中部地区包括山西省、安徽省、江西省、河南省、湖北省、湖南省。西部地区包括内蒙古自治区、广西壮族自治区、重庆市、四川省、贵州省、云南省、西藏自治区、陕西省、甘肃省、青海省、宁夏回族自治区、新疆维吾尔自治区。东北地区包括辽宁省、吉林省、黑龙江省。

3. 部分数据因四舍五入的原因,存在着与分项合计不等的情况。

“三农”发展举世瞩目 乡村振兴任重道远

——第三次全国农业普查结果显示“三农”发生历史性变革

国务院第三次全国农业普查领导小组副组长
国家统计局局长 宁吉喆

党的十九大报告提出必须始终把解决好“三农”问题作为全党工作重中之重，实施乡村振兴战略，为新时代“三农”发展指明了方向，提供了遵循。在全国上下不断掀起深入学习贯彻落实十九大精神热潮之际，历时三年多的第三次全国农业普查主要工作已顺利完成，主要普查结果为全面准确把握“三农”基本国情、实施乡村振兴战略提供了重要统计支撑。第三次全国农业普查结果显示，十年来尤其是党的十八大以来，在习近平新时代中国特色社会主义思想指引下，在党中央、国务院的坚强正确领导下，农业支持保护政策体系不断完善，强农惠农富农政策力度不断加大，现代农业建设成就辉煌，农村面貌和环境明显改善，农民生活质量显著提高，为决胜全面建成小康社会和实施乡村振兴战略奠定了坚实基础。

一、现代农业建设成就辉煌

实现乡村振兴，产业兴旺是基础。习近平总书记多次强调，中国要强，农业必须强。近年来尤其是党的十八大以来，党中央、国务院高度重视“三农”工作，采取一系列政策措施，持续加大对农业的支持保护力度，加强农业基础设施建设，提高农业物质技术装备水平，夯实农业基础，确保国家粮食安全和大宗农产品基本供给；以农业供给侧结构性改革为主线，调整优化农业产业产品结构，推动农业提质增效，提高竞争力；不断深化农村改革，实施土地“三权分置”改革，推进土地确权颁证，完善土地产权制度，培育新型农业生产经营主体，增强农业发展活力，提供坚强制度保障；转变农业增长方式，扎实推进现代农业建设。

(一)农业综合生产能力显著增强。确保十三亿多人的吃饭问题始终都是治国理政的头等大事。习近平总书记反复强调,"要把中国人的饭碗牢牢端在自己手中,我们的饭碗应该主要装中国粮"。近年来,我国农业综合生产能力显著增强,确保国家粮食安全和大宗农产品基本供给的能力明显提高。全国粮食总产量2006年低于10000亿斤,2013年首次突破12000亿斤大关,2014—2017年连续四年稳定在12000亿斤以上,粮食综合生产能力跃上新台阶,确保了国家粮食安全。全国肉类总产量和水产品总产量稳居世界第一。主要经济作物棉花、油料、糖料、蔬菜、水果等保持较高产量水平,为保障大宗农产品基本供给奠定了坚实基础。

(二)农田水利条件明显改善。完善的农业基础设施是提高农业综合生产能力的根本保障,也是现代农业发展水平的重要标志。第三次全国农业普查结果显示,我国农田水利条件明显改善,抵御自然灾害的能力增强。2016年末全国能够正常使用的机电井和排灌站比2006年末分别增长8.2%和8.9%,能够正常使用的灌溉用水塘和水库数量合计增长53.3%。2016年灌溉耕地面积占实际耕种耕地面积的比重达到55.2%,夯实了农业生产基础。

(三)农业机械化达到较高水平。农业机械拥有量较快增长,广泛应用,不仅极大地提高了农业劳动生产率,也逐步把农民从历史上"面朝黄土,背朝天"的高强度农业生产劳动中解放了出来。第三次全国农业普查结果显示,2016年末全国联合收获机114万台,比2006年末增长105.3%;排灌动力机械1431万台,增长6.1%。三大粮食作物达到较高机械化水平,小麦机耕、机播和机收的比重分别达到94.5%、82.0%和92.2%;玉米机耕、机播和机收的比重分别为73.7%、69.9%和61.7%;稻谷机耕、机播和机收的比重分别为83.3%、29.0%和80.1%。

(四)设施农业快速发展。大棚、温室等农业设施较快增长,改变了农业生产的时空分布,满足了人民日益增长的多样化需求。第三次全国农业普查结果显示,2016年末全国温室占地面积334千公顷,比2006年末增长312.6%,大棚占地面积981千公顷,增长111.0%。我国温室大棚占地面积稳居世界第一,工厂化种养也呈快速发展态势。

(五)农业生产经营人员文化素质提高。农村劳动力转移就业加快,市民化进程稳步推进,农业生产经营人员数量减少。据第三次全国农业普查结果,2016年全国从事农业生产经营管理活动一个月以上的人员数量为3.14亿人,比2006年下降8.7%。农业生产经营人员文化素质提高。2016年,初中文化程度的农业生产经营人员占比为48.4%,比2006年提高3.3个百分点;高中或中专文化程度的为7.1%,提高3.0个百分点;大专及以上的为1.2%,提高1.0个百分点。

(六)新型农业生产经营主体大量涌现。新型农业生产经营主体是现代农业建设的主导力量。近年来,国家在基础设施建设、工商、财政、税收、金融保险、用地等方面加大扶持力度,着力培育各类新型农业生产经营主体,农民专业合作社、家庭农场、农业企业等大量涌现。第三次全国农业普查结果显示,2016年末全国农业经营单位达到204万个,比2006年增长417.4%。农民专业合作社几乎从无到有,快速发展,提高了农业生产经营的组织化程度。2016年末以农业生产经营或服务为主的农民专业合作社达到 91 万个。

（七）适度规模经营发展迅速。根据第三次全国农业普查结果，2016 年耕地规模化耕种面积占全部实际耕地耕种面积的比重为 28.6%。其中，规模农业经营户所占比重为 17.0%；农业经营单位所占比重为 11.6%。规模化养殖生猪存栏占全国生猪存栏总数的比重为 62.9%，家禽存栏占比达到 73.9%。规模经营的快速发展对稳定农业生产、稳定农产品供应、稳定农产品市场都发挥了重要积极作用。

二、农村面貌和环境明显改善

中国要美，农村必须美。近年来国家加大农村基础设施力度，农村水电路气房等基础设施条件明显改善，大力推进农村环境整治，美丽宜居乡村建设稳步推进，农村面貌和环境明显改善。

（一）乡、村组织数量减少。随着城镇化进程加快推进，乡、村组织数量减少。第三次全国农业普查结果显示，2016 年末全国乡镇 31925 个，比 2006 年减少 8.1%；村委会和涉农居委会 596450 个，减少 6.4%；自然村 317 万个，减少 3.8%。

（二）农村基础设施明显改善。国家统筹城乡发展，着力加强农村基础设施建设，农村基础设施明显改善。第三次全国农业普查结果显示，2016 年末全国通公路的村占全部村的比重达到 99.3%，比 2006 年提高 3.8 个百分点；通村主要道路为水泥路面的村所占比重为 76.4%，提高 41.2 个百分点；村内主要道路为水泥路面的村比重为 80.9%，提高 53.2 个百分点；村内主要道路有路灯的村比重为 61.9%，提高 40.1 个百分点。通电的村所占比重为 99.7%，提高 1 个百分点；通电话的村比重为 99.5%，提高 1.9 个百分点；安装有线电视的村比重为 82.8%，提高 25.4 个百分点；接近 9 成的村通宽带互联网。有 73.9%的村生活垃圾集中处理或部分集中处理，提高 58.1 个百分点。

（三）农村基本社会服务全面进步。2016 年末，全国有幼儿园、托儿所的村占全部村的比重为 32.3%，比 2006 年提高 2.2 个百分点。有体育健身场所的村所占比重为 59.2%，提高 48.5 个百分点。有农民业余文化组织的村比重为 41.3%，提高 26.2 个百分点。有卫生室的村比重为 81.9%，提高 7.6 个百分点。

（四）农村新产业新业态蓬勃发展。2016 年，全国开展旅游接待的村占全部村的比重为 4.9%，比 2006 年提高 2.7 个百分点。农村电商由无到有，2016 年全国超过 1/4 的村有电子商务配送站点，有 4.4 万规模农业经营户和 5.1 万个农业经营单位通过电子商务销售农产品。规模农业经营户和农业经营单位从事设施农业的分别有 48.6 万户和 13.1 万个，从事循环农业生产的分别有 12.6 万户和 7.2 万个，从事工厂化生产的分别有 1.8 万户和 2.5 万个。大量返乡下乡人员在农村创业创新，为农村发展增添了新的活力。

三、农民生活质量和水平显著提高

中国要富，农民必须富。十九大报告强调，人民对美好生活的向往是我们党的奋斗目标，增进民生福祉是发展的根本目的。近年来尤其是党的十八大以来，国家多措并举，深挖农业内部增收潜力，拓宽农民增收渠道，农民收入快速增长，农民生活质量显著提高，广大人民群众的获得感、幸福感显著增强。

（一）农民收入持续快速增长。据城乡住户调查结果，2016 年农村居民人均可支配收入达到 12363 元，比 2012 年增长 47.4%，实际增长 36.3%，年均实际增长 8.0%。十八大以来，农村居民人均可支配收入年均实际增速比城镇居民高 1.5 个百分点，城乡居民收入增长差距扩大的趋势成功实现逆转。2016 年城乡居民人均可支配收入之比为 2.72（农村居民收入为 1），比 2012 年下降 0.16。农村居民恩格尔系数为 32.2%，比 2012 年下降 5.3 个百分点，农民生活水平不断提高。

（二）农户住房条件改善。据第三次全国农业普查结果，2016 年末 99.5%的农户拥有自己的住房，比 2006 年提高 0.2 个百分点。其中，拥有 1 处住房的农户占比为 87.0%，下降 5.5 个百分点；拥有 2 处和 3 处住房的农户所占比重分别为 11.6%和 0.9%，分别提高 5.2 个百分点和 0.5 个百分点；拥有商品房的农户达到 1997 万户，占全部农户的比重为 8.7%，而 10 年前很少有农户购买商品房。有 57.2%的农户住房为砖混结构，比 2006 年提高 17.8 个百分点；钢筋混凝土结构的占 12.5%，提高 6.5 个百分点；砖（石）木结构和竹草土坯结构的分别占 26.0%和 2.8%，分别下降 18.3 个百分点和 6.8 个百分点。

（三）饮用水更加安全。随着农村饮水安全工程的持续推进，农村饮水安全显著改善。根据第三次全国农业普查结果，2016 年全国有近 1.1 亿农户饮用经过净化处理的自来水，占全部农户比重为 47.7%，比 2006 年提高 24.6 个百分点。

（四）做饭取暖使用能源更加清洁。随着农村基础设施条件逐步改善，农民生活用能源结构发生较大变化，做饭取暖使用能源由历史上主要使用柴草和煤为主，逐渐转变为使用电、天然气、液化石油气等更为清洁的能源，生活方式更为绿色生态。2016 年，农户做饭取暖[①]主要使用电的有 13503 万户，占 58.6%，比 2006 年提高 57.8 个百分点；主要使用煤气、天然气、液化石油气的有 11347 万户，占 49.3%，提高 37.4 个百分点。

（五）卫生设施条件改善。2016 年，使用水冲式卫生厕所的农户有 8339 万户，占全部农户的比重为 36.2%；使用卫生旱厕的 2859 万户，占 12.4%。

（六）耐用消费品拥有数量增加。2016 年，全国平均每百户农户拥有小汽车 24.8 台，比 2006 年增加 21.4 台；彩色电视机 115.2 台，增加 27.9 台；电脑 32.2 台，增加 30.0 台；手机 244.3 部，增加 174.5 部。

在习近平新时代中国特色社会主义思想指引下，在党中央、国务院正确领导下，在各地区各部门共同努力下，十年来尤其是党的十八大以来，"三农"发生了历史性变革，现代农业建设取得辉煌成就，农村面貌和环境明显改善，农民生活质量显著提高，但也要清醒地认识到农业现代化仍是"四化同步"的短板，农村仍是全面建成小康社会的短腿，发展不平衡不充分的问题尤为突出。让我们紧密团结在以习近平同志为核心的党中央周围，以习近平新时代中国特色社会主义思想为统领，贯彻落实新发展理念，坚定实施乡村振兴战略，妥善化解各种风险挑战，为决胜全面建成小康社会，夺取新时代中国特色社会主义伟大胜利而不懈努力奋斗。

---

① 此指标每户可选两项，分项占比之和超过 100%。

Communique of the Third National Agricultural Census (No. 1)

The Steering Group Office of the Third National Agricultural Census of the State Council
National Bureau of Statistics of China
December 14, 2017

In order to collect basic information of agriculture, rural areas and farmers across the country, identify new developments and new changes related to these three issues, the State Council carried out the third national agricultural census based on reference day of December 31, 2016 and reference period of year 2016. The census covered household-based agricultural operators, rural households holding a land contract with the state collective or possess the means of agricultural production, agricultural enterprises, villagers' committees and town and township governments. The census was designed to collect information on agricultural production capacity, agriculture outputs, agriculture infrastructure and its basic social services and living situation of farmers, etc. The agricultural census was a nationwide complete enumeration. The enumerators interviewed each respondent and filled out questionnaires. The census, engaging nearly 4 million personnel, including enumerators, census supervisors and staff members of related agencies at all levels, covering 230 million farmers, 600,000 village-level units, 40,000 township-level units and over 2 million agricultural operational holdings. More than 50,000 staff members participated in the measurement of the sown area of grain, cotton and other staple crops using satellite remote sensing technology, more than 100,000 scenes of satellite remote sensing data was processed. 110,000 sample segments and over

20,000 selected census areas were surveyed. More than 2,700 aerial surveys using unmanned aerial vehicles were conducted for entire coverage of sample villages, collecting data on the spatial distribution of major crops all over the country, as well as the planting area of major crops production counties in each province(autonomous region/municipality).

In accordance with international practice, the Steering Group Office of the Third National Agricultural Census of the State Council conducted post-enumeration sample survey for quality assessments. The assessment results show that the percentage of coverage omission of registered households was 0. 19%, the difference rate of census data was 0. 40%, which fulfil the designed data quality standard.

According to the *Regulations on the National Agricultural Census*, the Steering Group Office of the Third National Agricultural Census of the State Council and the National Bureau of Statistics will release the results of the census in forms of bulletin.

Basic Information on the Agriculture, Rural Areas and Farmers

The Third National Agricultural Census enumerated 31, 925 towns and townships (11,081 townships and 20,844 towns), 596,450 villages (including 556,264 villager committees and 40,186 agriculture-related neighborhood committees), 3,170,000 natural villages, and 150,000 rural settlements established after year 2006.

I. Agricultural Entities

In 2016, there were 2. 04 million agricultural holdings nationwide. As of the end of 2016, the number of farmer cooperatives registered in the industrial and commercial authority up to 1. 79 million, of which 910,000 farmer cooperatives mainly engaged in agricultural production and services. There were 207. 43 million household-based agricultural operators, of which 3. 98 million were large-scale operators/households. There were 314. 22 million agriculture operators in China.

II. Ownership of Agricultural Machinery

As of the end of 2016, there were 26. 9 million tractors, 5. 13 million rotary tillers, 8. 25 million rotary cultivators, 6. 52 million seeding machines, 680,000 rice transplanters, 1. 14 million combine harvesters and threshers and 10. 31 million power threshers.

III. Use of Land

As of the end of 2016, the area of cropland in China[①] was 134, 921 thousand hectares. The actual operation area of forests (excluding ecological forests and shelterbelts that are not included in the compensation area for ecological forests) was 203,046 thousand hectares and that of pasture/grassland was 224,388 thousand hectares.

IV. Rural Infrastructure

As of the end of 2016, 8.6% of the total townships and towns had railway stations; 7.7% had docks; 21.5% had expressway entrances and exits; and 99.3% had roads to villages.

As of the end of 2016, there were 99.7% of the villages in the country where electricity is available and 11.9% of the villages had access to natural gas supply services. 25.1% villages had distribution sites for e-commerce platforms.

As of the end of 2016, 91.3% of all townships and towns had access to centralized or partially centralized water supply services and 90.8% of all townships and towns had access to centralized or partially centralized garbage management services. 73.9% villages had access to centralized or partially centralized garbage management services. 17.4% villages had access to centralized or partially centralized domestic wastewater treatment services. 53.5% villages completed or partially completed the toilet upgrading.

V. Basic Public Services

As of the end of 2016, 96.8% townships and towns had libraries and cultural centers; 11.9% townships and towns had theaters or cinemas; 16.6% townships and towns had stadiums; 70.6% townships and towns had parks and recreational squares. 59.2% villages had fitness facilities.

As of the end of 2016, 96.5% townships and towns had nurseries and kindergartens and 98.0% had primary schools. 32.3% villages had nurseries and kindergartens.

As of the end of 2016, 99.9% townships and towns had health care facilities; 98.4% had practicing (assistant) physicians; and 66.8% had social welfare institutions. 81.9% villages

---

① Data for cultivated land came from the Ministry of Land and Resources.

had clinics.

VI. Living Situation of Farmers

As of the end of 2016, 99.5% of Chinese rural households owned their own dwellings; 47.7% rural households had access to purified tap water;36.2% used water-flushed toilets.

Notes:

1. Township/town: administrative units, including key towns and non-key towns and townships, excluding community offices at sub-district or township/town-level regulatory government agencies for farming, forestry, animal husbandry and fishery.

2. Village: area under jurisdiction of a villager committee or an agriculture-related neighborhood committee.

3. Natural village: a rural settlement formed through a natural process. A natural village generally has a name.

4. Household-based agricultural operator: rural households involved in farming, forestry, animal husbandry, fishery and related service activities in the People's Republic of China (excluding Hong Kong, Macau and Taiwan).

5. Large-sale household-based agricultural operator: refers to the agricultural operational household that has a great scale of commercialized agriculture business. The agricultural operational household that meets one of the following requirements is registered as the large scale household:

Crop farming: the crops cultivated in the open fields of single cropping system area are up to 100 mu and more, the crops cultivated in the open fields of double cropping system area are up to 50 mu and more, and the facilities used in the facility agriculture area cover an area of 25 mu and more;

Livestock: 200 and more pigs are ready for slaughtering every year; 20 and more beef cattle are ready for slaughtering every year; 20 and more dairy cattle are in inventory; 100 and more sheep are ready for slaughtering every year; 10,000 and more broiler chickens and meat ducks are ready for slaughtering every year; 2,000 and more laying hens and ducks are in inventory; 1,000 and more gooses are ready for slaughtering every year;

Forestry: the area of woodland operated is up to 500 mu and more;

Aquaculture and fisheries: the freshwater and marine aquaculture area is up to 50 mu and more; 1 and more fishing powerboats with the minimum length of 24 m are owned; 2 and more fishing powerboats with the minimum length of 12 m are owned; the revenue from other fisheries businesses is up to 300,000 RMB and more;

Services for agriculture: the operating revenue from services for crop farming, forestry, livestock and fishery for other households is up to 100,000 RMB and more.

Others: The agricultural households that fail to reach any requirement above but have the annual sales of various agricultural products of crop farming, forestry, livestock and fishery up to 100,000 RMB and more, like various large specialized farming and planting households, are registered as large scale households.

6. Agricultural holdings: legal entities and unregistered entities mainly involved in agricultural production and service activities as well as agricultural establishments of whose entities are not primarily engaged in agricultural activities within the territory of the People's Republic of China (not including Hong Kong, Macau and Taiwan in census), including crop farms, tree farms, livestock farms, fishing farms, units involving in services related to farming, forestry, animal husbandry or fishery, farmer cooperatives involved in agricultural operation activities; and agricultural establishments subordinated to relevant government agencies, non-government organizations, education institutions, research institutions, manufacturing and mining enterprises, villager committees, neighborhood committees, foundations and so on.

7. Agriculture operators: the number of employed persons (including persons employed on a part-time basis) who have engaged in agricultural production and service activities for more than 30 days in agricultural operation households or other agricultural holdings.

8. Farmer cooperative: a cooperative where farmers pool their resources in agricultural production or related service activities. Farmer cooperatives should comply with the provisions of the *Farmer Cooperative Law* on the nature of cooperatives, the conditions and procedures for establishment, rights and obligations of members, organizational and financial management and "farmer cooperative" must be specified in the name of the entities. They include farmer cooperatives which have registered with the industrial and commercial authority and unregistered farmer cooperatives that meet the above requirements, but do not include joint-stock cooperative enterprises, community-based economic cooperatives, supply and marketing cooperatives, rural credit cooperatives and other cooperatives registered with a corporate name. Cooperatives of farmers engaged in non-agricultural industries such as purchase of agricultural assets or processing, storage, transportation, and sale of agricultural products are excluded.

9. Tractor: a tractor with an engine rated at more than 2. 2 kw (inclusive), including small four-wheel and walk-behind tractors.

10. Rotary tiller: engine-powered machine used to prepare paddy or dry fields, including micro tillers and pastoral farming machine.

11. Rotary cultivator: machine used with a tractor to complete plowing and raking activities.

12. Seeding machine: including seeding machine with different types of drills, each with their specific working mechanisms, characteristics and suitability for sowing certain types of seeds.

13. Rice transplanter: engine-powered machine fitted to plant rice seedlings onto paddy field.

14. Combine harvester and thresher: machine that can be used for multiple purposes, including harvesting, threshing, separation, cleaning and many other processes, including multi-purpose rice harvesters and multi-purpose coin harvesters.

15. Power thresher: engine-powered machine used for crop threshing.

16. Operational area of woodland: the total area of woodland managed by household-based agricultural operators and agricultural entities during the reference period. Woodland is land where trees, bamboo, shrubs, and

mangrove are planted and managed for timber production, including cutover land, but not including vegetated residential land, vegetated land designated for railways and roads, vegetated embankments of rivers and ditches, or ecological forests and shelterbelts excluded in the compensation area for ecological forests.

17. Operational area of pasture (grassland): the total area of pasture (grassland) managed household-based agricultural operators and agricultural entities during the reference period. Pasture is land used for grazing and the vegetation of pasture consists mainly of herbs.

18. Townships and towns with railway stations: townships and towns with sites where trains stop to pick up or let off passengers or goods. The establishment of a rail station must be approved by the state railway authority.

19. Townships and towns with docks: townships and towns with structures extending along shore or out from the shore into a body of water, including sea, rivers, lakes and reservoir, to which boats may be moored for the loading and unloading of passengers and goods, excluding docks in parks.

20. Townships and towns with expressway entrances and exits: townships and towns with entrances and exits of expressways that meet the requirements of the *Technical Standards for Highway Engineering* issued by the Ministry of Transport.

21. Villages with distribution sites for e-commerce platforms: villages with distribution stations for online shopping platforms and other new business mode.

22. Townships and towns with access to centralized or partially centralized water supply: townships/towns where all or some residents have access to tap water.

23. Villages with access to centralized or partially centralized garbage management services: villages with centralized garbage disposal facilities or villages where there are no such facilities but garbage was collected and disposed in accordance with a centralized management plan.

24. Villages with access to centralized or partially centralized domestic wastewater treatment services: villages with centralized wastewater treatment facilities or villages where there are no such facilities but wastewater was collected and disposed in accordance with a centralized treatment plan.

25. Villages which completed or partially completed the toilet upgrading: villages which have converted all or part of its open-air pit toilets, cesspools, dry toilets and simple toilets to toilets with septic tanks, digesters or three-compartment tanks. Some residents use public toilets or dump excreta to other designated places.

26. Townships and towns with libraries and cultural centers: townships and towns with public libraries and cultural centers approved by the cultural administration authority, excluding libraries affiliated to other entities.

27. Townships and towns with theaters or cinemas: townships and towns with theaters or cinemas in which plays and other dramatic performance are given and films are shown, as authorized by the cultural administration authority, including theaters and cinemas as independent accounting units as well as affiliated theaters open to the public.

28. Townships and townswith sport venues : townships and towns with sport venues under their jurisdiction. A sport venue here is an outdoor stadium consisting of a football field surrounded by a 400-meter track. It should have

fixed curbs, more than 6 runways and grandstand seats. A stadium refers to an indoor venue with bleachers, used to host basketball, volleyball, badminton, table tennis, gymnastics and other sport events. Sport venues and stadiums affiliated to schools, enterprises or government agencies and open to the public are covered in the census and fitness squares are not covered.

29. Townships and towns with parks and recreational squares: townships and towns with places where residents can relax and play. These places must be approved by the relevant authority.

30. Villages with fitness facilities: villages with fitness centers, sport venues or stadiums which are built by village authorities, individuals or other institutions for serving the public.

31. Township/towns/villages with kindergartens or nurseries: township/towns/villages with kindergartens or nurseries, including preschool education classes and non-licensed, privately-run kindergartens or nurseries with more than 10 children, under their jurisdiction.

32. Townships and towns with primary schools: townships and towns with schools which have been approved by an education authority at or above the county level and offer primary education programs for children of primary school age.

33. Townships and towns with health care facilities: townships and towns with facilities which have obtained the Practice License of Medical Institution of the People's Republic of China and the Permit for Family Planning Technical Services from the public health administrative authority, or obtain a legal entity registration certificate from the administrative authorities for civil affairs, industry and commerce, and institution-setup and are authorized to provide health care, disease control, health supervision services or medical research and on-the-job medical training, including hospitals, grass-roots health care facilities, professional public health agencies and other medical and health facilities.

34. Townships and towns with practicing (assistant) physicians: townships and towns with one or more practicing physicians or practicing assistant physicians who have practicing certificates for registered doctors and are engaged in disease control and prevention. Physicians who have practicing certificates but are engaged in management activities are not included.

35. Townships and towns with social welfare institutions: townships and towns with not-for-profit institutions that provide accommodation for profit for people in difficulty, including various veteran homes, charity homes, children's homes, facility for the mentally challenged, homes for the elderly and nursing homes.

36. Villages with clinics: villages with clinics/health care facilities established by entities or individuals and licensed by a health care authority at or above the county level. Such clinics/health care facilities must have a fixed place of business and are mainly engaged in health care activities. Dental clinics and units that are primarily engaged in drug sale are not included.

37. Dwelling: a building for human habitation, with walls, a roof, doors, windows and other structures. They can protect people from rain and wind. Caves, bamboo huts, yurts, tents, houseboats and other special local dwell-

ings are also included.

38. Purified tap water: water that is purified and sanitized by water plants or centralized decontamination facilities and complies with national drinking water standards.

39. Water-flush toilet(flushed into the sewers, septic tanks and toilet pits): toilets which have water supply and drainage system or a bucket (with a scoop) and dispose excreta by using water to flush it to the sewers, septic tanks or toilet pits, including sitting and squatting toilets, with or without water seals. They won't attract flies or cause environmental pollution.

Communique of the Third National Agricultural Census (No. 2)

Agricultural Entities, Agricultural Machinery and Facilities

The Steering Group Office of the Third National Agricultural Census of the State Council
National Bureau of Statistics of China
December 15, 2017

The Third National Agricultural Census enumerated agricultural entities, agricultural machinery and facilities across the country. The Census results are as follows:

I. Number of Agricultural Entities

In 2016, China had 207.43 million household-based agricultural holdings, of which 3.98 million were large-scale agricultural households. There were 2.04 million agricultural enterprises. As of the end of 2016, the total number of farmer cooperatives registered in the industrial and commercial authority was 1.79 million, of which 910,000 were farmer cooperatives mainly engaged in agricultural production or service.

Table 1 Number of Agricultural Entities

Unit: 10,000

Items	Nationwide	East China	Central China	West China	Northeast China
Household-based agricultural holdings	20743	6479	6427	6647	1190
# Large-scale agricultural households	398	119	86	110	83
Agricultural entities	204	69	56	62	17
# Farmer cooperatives	91	32	27	22	10

Note: Farmer cooperatives are farmer cooperatives mainly engaged in agricultural production and service.

II. Agricultural Machinery

As of the end of 2016, there were 26. 9 million tractors, 5. 13 million tillage machines, 8. 25 million rotary cultivators, 1. 14 million combine harvesters and threshers, 6. 52 million seeding machines, 14. 31 million power-driven irrigation and drainage machines.

Table 2 Number of Major Agricultural Machinery

Unit: 10,000

Items	Nationwide	East China	Central China	West China	Northeast China
Tractors	2690	758	888	582	463
Rotary tillers	513	70	163	240	40
Rotary cultivators	825	148	183	430	65
Seeding machines	652	108	258	126	160
Rice transplanters	68	9	11	6	42
Power-driven Irrigation and drainage machines	1431	442	521	384	84
Combine harvesters and threshers	114	33	45	16	20
Power threshers	1031	134	271	600	26
Processing machines of composite feed	409	23	37	303	46
Milking machines	10	2	1	5	2
Wool shearing machines	5	1	1	2	0. 5
Oxygen-increasing machines	194	125	42	23	3
Fruit tree pruning machine	49	21	13	14	0. 6
Motorized fishing boats for inland water bodies	28	13	10	3	1
Motorized fishing boats for sea	25	22	0. 0	1	2

III. Cropland Water Conservation Facilities

As of the end of 2016, the number of electromechanical wells was 6. 59 million, irrigation and drainage stations was 0. 42 million, irrigation ponds and reservoirs that could be normally used was 3. 49 million.

Table 3 Cropland Water Conservation Facilities

Unit: 10,000

Items	Nationwide	East China	Central China	West China	Northeast China
Usable electromechanical wells	659	206	208	152	92
Irrigation and drainage stations	42	18	16	7	1
Usable irrigation ponds and reserviors	349	43	224	78	4

As of the end of 2016, there were 61.89 million hectares of irrigated cropland in the country, of which 10.018 million hectares of cropland using sprinkler irrigation systems, drip irrigation systems and infiltration irrigation systems. 30.5% of rural households and agricultural production holdings mainly used groundwater for irrigation and 69.5% mainly used surface water for irrigation.

Table 4 Cropland Irrigation

Unit: 1,000 hectares, %

Items	Nationwide	East China	Central China	West China	Northeast China
Area of irrigated cropland	61890	16044	20064	18633	7148
# Area of cropland with sprinkler irrigation systems, drip irrigation systems and infiltration irrigation systems	10018	1655	1899	5079	1385
Primary water source for irrigation					
Ground water	30.5	36.9	35.7	12.1	59.3
Surface water	69.5	63.1	64.3	87.9	40.7

IV. Facility Agriculture

As of the end of 2016, the aggregate area of greenhouses in China reached 334,000 hectares, the area covered by plastic nurseries was 981,000 hectares and the area of fishing farms was 7,600 hectares.

Table 5 Facility Agriculture

Unit: 1,000 hectares

Items	Nationwide	East China	Central China	West China	Northeast China
Area of greenhouses	334	130	41	95	69
Area of plastic nurseries	981	474	186	215	106
Area of fishing farms	7.6	4.5	1.7	1.0	0.3

Notes:

1. Household-based agricultural holdings: rural households engaged in crop farming, forestry, animal husbandry, fishery and related service activities within the territory of the People's Republic of China (excluding Hong Kong,

Macau and Taiwan in census).

2. Large-scale agricultural households: refers to the agricultural operation households that has larger scale commercialized agricultural products. The criteria are:

Crop farming: the crops cultivated in the open fields of single cropping system area are up to 100 mu and more, the crops cultivated in the open fields of double cropping system area are up to 50 mu and more, and the facilities used in the facility agriculture area cover an area of 25 mu and more;

Animal husbandry: 200 and more pigs are ready for slaughtering every year; 20 and more beef cattle are ready for slaughtering every year; 20 and more dairy cattle are on hand; 100 and more sheep are ready for slaughtering every year; 10,000 and more broiler chickens and meat ducks are ready for slaughtering every year; 2,000 and more laying hens and ducks are on hand; 1,000 and more gooses are ready for slaughtering every year;

Forestry: the woodland area is up to 500 mu and more;

Aquaculture and fisheries: the freshwater or marine aquaculture area is up to 50 mu and more; with 1 and more 24-meter fishing powerboats; with 2 and more 12-meter fishing powerboats; the revenue from other fishery businesses is up to 300,000 RMB and above;

Services for crop farming, forestry, animal husbandry and fishery: the operating revenue from services for crop farming, forestry, livestock and aquaculture and fisheries for other households is up to 100,000 RMB and above.

Others: The agricultural households that fail to reach any one of the above criteria requirement above but have the annual sales of various agricultural products of crop farming, forestry, animal husbandry and fishery up to 100,000 RMB and above, e. g. various large specialized farming and planting households.

3. Agricultural holdings: legal entities and unregistered entities mainly involved in agricultural production and service activities as well as agricultural establishments of whose entities are not primarily engaged in agricultural activities within the territory of the People's Republic of China (not including Hong Kong, Macau and Taiwan in census), including crop farms, tree farms, livestock farms, fishing farms, units involving in services related to farming, forestry, animal husbandry or fishery, farmer cooperatives involved in agricultural operation activities; and agricultural establishments subordinated to relevant government agencies, non-government organizations, education institutions, research institutions, manufacturing and mining enterprises, villager committees, neighborhood committees, foundations and so on.

4. Farmer cooperatives: Farmer cooperative, as an economic organization for farmers' reciprocity and in the name of "farmer cooperative", should comply with the provisions of the *Farmer Cooperative Law* on the nature of cooperatives, the conditions and procedures for establishment, rights and obligations of members, organizational and financial management, and shall has agricultural operation or services related to crop farming, forestry, animal husbandry and fishery. It includes those farmer cooperatives registered with the industrial and commercial authority and those unregistered farmer cooperatives that meet the above requirements, but do not include joint-stock cooperative enterprises, community-based economic cooperatives, supply and marketing cooperatives, rural credit cooperatives

and other cooperatives registered with a corporate name. Cooperatives of farmers engaged in non-agricultural industries such as purchase of agricultural assets or processing, storage, transportation, and sale of agricultural products are not included either.

5. Tractor: a tractor with an engine rated more than 2.2 kw (inclusive), including small four-wheel and walking tractors.

6. Rotary tiller: engine-powered machine used to prepare paddy or dry fields, including micro tillers and pastoral farming machine.

7. Rotary cultivator: machine used with a tractor to complete plowing and raking activities.

8. Seeding machine: including seeding machine with different types of drills, each with their specific working mechanisms, characteristics and suitability for sowing certain types of seeds.

9. Rice transplanter: engine-powered machine fitted to plant rice seedlings onto paddy field.

10. Combine harvester and thresher: machine that can be used for multiple purposes, including harvesting, threshing, separation, cleaning and many other processes, including multi-purpose rice harvesters and multi-purpose coin harvesters.

11. Power thresher: engine-powered machine used for crop threshing.

12. Area of irrigatedcropland: cultivated cropland with irrigation facilities and water sources and is irrigable under normal climate.

13. Area of greenhouses and plastic nurseries: consisting of three parts: (i) floor area within the inner boundaries of walls; (ii) the area covered by walls and other supporting structures; and (iii) area required for lighting, which refers to the area within necessary distance from light-shielding objects (other facilities, houses, etc.).

14. Four regions: East China includes Beijing Municipality, Tianjin Municipality, Hebei Province, Shanghai Municipality, Jiangsu Province, Zhejiang Province, Fujian Province, Shandong Province, Guangdong Province and Hainan Province. Central China includes Shanxi Province, Anhui Province, Jiangxi Province, Henan Province, Hubei Province and Hunan Province. West China includes Inner Mongolia Autonomous Region, Guangxi Zhuang Autonomous Region, Chongqing Municipality, Sichuan Province, Guizhou Province, Yunnan Province, Tibet Autonomous Region, Shaanxi Province, Gansu Province, Qinghai Province, Ningxia Hui Autonomous Region and Xinjiang Uygur Autonomous Region. Northeast China includes Liaoning Province, Jilin Province and Heilongjiang Province.

15. Because of rounding after the decimal point, sums of individual items may not equal to the total.

Communique of the Third National Agricultural Census (No. 3)

Rural Infrastructure and Basic Public Services

The Steering Group Office of the Third National Agricultural Census of the State Council
National Bureau of Statistics of China
December 15, 2017

The Third National Agricultural Census enumerated the conditions of infrastructure and basic public services in 31,925 towns and townships as well as 596,450 villages. The following are the main census results:

I. Transportation

As of the end of 2016, 8.6% towns and townships had railway stations; 7.7% had docks; 21.5% had expressway entrances and exits.

99.3% villages had access to the nationwide highway network, 61.9% had main roads with street lamps. In most villages, the distance between the farthest natural village or residential settlement to the villager committee was within 5 km.

Table 1 Rural Transportation Infrastructure

Unit: %

Items	Nationwide	East China	Central China	West China	Northeast China
Townships/towns with railway stations	8. 6	7. 6	8. 3	7. 7	18. 0
Townships/towns with docks	7. 7	10. 0	8. 5	6. 7	3. 3
Townships/towns with expressway entrances and exits	21. 5	28. 9	22. 6	17. 0	19. 9
Villages with access to highways	99. 3	99. 9	99. 5	98. 3	99. 7
Type of roads connecting the village to a town/township					
# Cement roads	76. 4	76. 4	86. 1	70. 2	59. 3
Asphalt road	20. 2	22. 2	12. 3	22. 5	35. 1
Gravel road	2. 3	0. 6	1. 0	5. 3	3. 5
Type of main roads inside the village					
# Cement roads	80. 9	84. 0	89. 7	72. 7	60. 0
Asphalt road	8. 6	11. 1	3. 4	9. 0	15. 9
Gravel road	6. 7	2. 4	4. 7	11. 7	18. 9
Villages which had main roads with street lamps	61. 9	85. 9	59. 8	35. 5	54. 1
Distance from the farthest natural village or residential settlement to the villager committee					
Within 5 km	90. 8	97. 1	93. 0	80. 7	90. 9
6-20 km	6. 6	2. 3	5. 5	13. 0	7. 1
11-20 km	2. 0	0. 5	1. 3	4. 6	1. 6
Above 20 km	0. 6	0. 1	0. 2	1. 7	0. 4

II. Energy and Communication

99. 7% villages had access to electricity; natural gas 11. 9%; landline services 99. 5%; cable TV 82. 8%; and broadband services 89. 9%. 25. 1% villages had distribution sites for e-commerce platforms.

Table 2 Energy and Communication Infrastructure in Villages

Unit: %

Items	Nationwide	East China	Central China	West China	Northeast China
Electrified villages	99. 7	100. 0	99. 9	99. 2	100. 0
Villages with access to natural gas	11. 9	10. 3	8. 4	18. 3	4. 7
Villages with access to landlines	99. 5	100. 0	99. 7	98. 7	100. 0
Villages with access with cable TV	82. 8	94. 7	82. 9	65. 5	95. 7
Villages with access to broadband services	89. 9	97. 1	92. 7	77. 3	96. 5
Villages with distribution sites for e-commerce platforms	25. 1	29. 4	22. 9	21. 9	24. 1

III. Sanitary Conditions

As of the end of 2016, 91. 3% of the townships and towns had access to centralized or partially centralized water supply services, 90. 8% of the townships and towns had access to centralized or partially centralized garbage management services. 73. 9% villages had access to centralized or partially centralized garbage management services. 17. 4% villages had access to centralized or partially centralized domestic wastewater treatment services. 53. 5% villages completed or partially completed the toilet upgrading.

Table 3 Sanitary Facilities in Townships/Towns/Villages

Unit: %

Items	Nationwide	East China	Central China	West China	Northeast China
Townships and towns with access to centralized or partially centralized water supply	91. 3	96. 1	93. 1	87. 1	93. 6
Townships and towns with access to centralized or partially centralized garbage management services	90. 8	94. 6	92. 8	89. 0	82. 3
Villages with access to centralized or partially centralized garbage management services	73. 9	90. 9	69. 7	60. 3	53. 1
Villages with access to centralized or partially centralized wastewater treatment services	17. 4	27. 1	12. 5	11. 6	7. 8
Villages which completed or partially completed the toilet upgrading	53. 5	64. 5	49. 1	49. 1	23. 7

IV. Culture and Education

As of the end of 2016, 96. 5% townships and towns had nurseries and kindergartens, 98. 0% had primary schools, 96. 8% had libraries and cultural centers, 11. 9% had theaters and cinemas, 16. 6% had sport venues, and 70. 6% had parks and recreational squares.

32. 3% villages had nurseries and kindergartens, 59. 2% had fitness facilities; villages with recreational facilities were accounted for 41. 3%.

Table 4 Recreational and Educational Facilities in Townships/Towns/Villages

Unit: %

Items	Nationwide	East China	Central China	West China	Northeast China
Townships and towns with nurseries and kindergartens	96.5	98.7	98.3	94.0	96.9
Townships and towns with primary schools	98.0	98.7	99.5	97.3	95.2
Townships and towns with libraries or cultural centers	96.8	96.2	98.0	96.6	95.2
Townships and towns with theaters or cinemas	11.9	18.5	14.4	7.9	5.9
Townships and towns with sport venues	16.6	20.5	19.4	13.5	12.1
Townships and towns with parks and recreational squares	70.6	83.2	73.9	59.4	84.0
Villages with nurseries and kindergartens	32.3	29.6	36.5	33.0	25.8
Villages with fitness facilities	59.2	72.2	55.5	46.0	62.8
Villages with recreational facilities	41.3	44.4	40.8	36.7	47.1

V. Health Care and Social Welfare Institutions

As of the end of 2016, 99.9% townships and towns had health care facilities; 98.4% had practicing (assistant) physicians; 66.8% had social welfare institutions; 56.4% had nursing homes founded by the township/town-level government.

81.9% villages had clinics, 54.9% had practicing (assistant) physicians.

Table 5 Health Care and Social Welfare Institutions in Townships/Towns/Villages

Unit: %

Items	Nationwide	East China	Central China	West China	Northeast China
Townships and towns with health care facilities	99.9	99.9	100.0	99.8	99.7
Townships and towns with practicing (assistant) physicians	98.4	99.6	99.8	96.7	99.3
Townships and towns with social welfare institutions	66.8	71.7	87.7	53.3	57.0
Townships and towns with nursing homes founded by the township/town-level government	56.4	61.9	78.0	43.3	40.8
Villages with clinics	81.9	71.9	89.3	86.9	86.2
Villages with practicing (assistant) physicians	54.9	49.4	66.7	49.9	60.6

VI. Marketplaces

As of the end of 2016, 68.1% townships and towns had commodity markets; 39.4% had specialized markets selling grain, edible oil, vegetables and fruits; 10.8% had specialized livestock and poultry markets; 4.3% had specialized aquaculture markets.

47.5% of the villages had groceries or supermarkets that covered an area of more than 50 square meters; 4.9% of the villages were involved in tourism business; 30.0% villages had licensed restaurants.

Table 6 Marketplaces in Townships/Towns/Villages

Unit: %

Items	Nationwide	East China	Central China	West China	Northeast China
Townships/towns with marketplace	68.1	75.5	72.3	62.0	65.1
Townships/towns with specialized markets selling grain, edible oil, vegetables and fruits	39.4	40.2	43.8	36.2	40.7
Townships/towns with specialized livestock and poultry markets	10.8	7.7	12.9	12.2	5.0
Townships/towns with specialized aquaculture markets	4.3	5.3	7.2	2.5	1.7
Villages with groceries or supermarkets that covered an area of more than 50 square meters	47.5	50.2	54.8	34.0	65.6
Villages involved in tourism business	4.9	3.8	4.6	6.9	3.2
Villages with licensed restaurants	30.0	31.3	32.4	26.6	27.1

Notes:

1. Township/town: administrative unit, including key towns and non-key towns and townships, but not including subdistrict offices or township/town-level regulatory government agencies for agriculture, forestry, animal husbandry and fishery;

2. Village: area under jurisdiction of a villager committee or an agriculture-related neighborhood committee.

3. Villages with main roads with street lamps: villages where the village-level governance authorities or other units have installed street lamps on the main roads. Street lamps not include lamps installed in front of houses by farmers.

4. Villages with distribution centers for e-commerce platforms: villages with distribution stations for online shopping platforms and other new business modes.

5. Townships and towns with access to centralized or partially centralized water supply: townships/towns where all or some residents have access to tap water.

6. Villages with access to centralized or partially centralized garbage management services: villages with centralized garbage disposal facilities or villages where there are no such facilities but garbage is collected and disposed in accordance with a centralized management plan.

7. Villages which completed or partially completed the toilet upgrading: villages which have converted all or part of its open-air pit toilets, cesspools, dry toilets and simple toilets to toilets with septic tanks, digesters or three-com-

partment tanks. Some residents use public toilets or dump excreta to other designated places.

8. Townships and towns with social welfare institutions: townships and towns with not-for-profit institutions that provide accommodation for profit for people in difficulty, including various veteran homes, welfare homes, children's homes, facility for the mentally challenged, homes for the elderly and nursing homes.

9. Villages with clinics: villages with clinics/health care facilities established by entities or individuals and licensed by a health care authority at or above the county level. Such clinics/health care facilities must have a fixed place of business and are mainly engaged in health care activities. Dental clinics and the units that are primarily engaged in drug sale are excluded.

10. Villages involved in tourism business : villages where some residents are engaged in tourist reception, catering and accommodation service activities with a license within the villages, including farmers working at teahouses, pubs, countryside inns, farmhouses, etc. in the villages.

11. Townships and towns with marketplaces: townships and towns with public marketplaces where people can purchase and sell consumer goods, assets and other products and related services. Such marketplaces must have been licensed and regulated by relevant authorities and in operation on a regular basis or for at least three months.

12. Four regions: East China includes Beijing Municipality, Tianjin Municipality, Hebei Province, Shanghai Municipality, Jiangsu Province, Zhejiang Province, Fujian Province, Shandong Province, Guangdong Province and Hainan Province. Central China includes Shanxi Province, Anhui Province, Jiangxi Province, Henan Province, Hubei Province and Hunan Province. West China includes Inner Mongolia Autonomous Region, Guangxi Zhuang Autonomous Region, Chongqing Municipality, Sichuan Province, Guizhou Province, Yunnan Province, Tibet Autonomous Region, Shaanxi Province, Gansu Province, Qinghai Province, Ningxia Hui Autonomous Region and Xinjiang Uygur Autonomous Region. Northeast China includes Liaoning Province, Jilin Province and Heilongjiang Province.

13. Because of rounding after the decimal point, sums of individual items may not equal totals.

Communique of the Third National Agricultural Census (No. 4)

Living Conditions of Farmers

The Steering Group Office of the Third National Agricultural Census of the State Council
National Bureau of Statistics of China
December 16, 2017

The Third National Agricultural Census enumerated the living conditions of 230.27 million farmers. The following are the results of the census:

I. Housing

As of the end of 2016, 99.5% of rural households had their own dwellings. Among them, 200.3 million rural households had one dwelling, accounting for 87.0% of all rural households; 26.77 million rural households had two dwellings, accounting for 11.6%; 1.96 million rural households had three or more than three dwellings, accounting for 0.9%; 19.97 million rural households owned commercial residential flats, accounting for 8.7%.

Most dwellings of rural households had brick and concrete structure or brick (stone) wood structure. There were 131.82 million rural dwellings with brick and concrete structure, accounting for 57.2%; 59.93 million rural dwellings with brick (stone) wood structure, accounting for 26.0%; 28.84 million rural dwellings with concrete structure, accounting for

12.5%; 6.40 million rural dwellings with a bamboo-grass adobe structure, accounting for 2.8%; 3.29 million rural dwellings with other structures, accounting for 1.4%.

Table 1 Number and Structure of Dwellings

Unit: %, × 10000

Items	Nationwide	East China	Central China	West China	Northeast China
By the number of owned dwellings					
1 dwellings	87.0	82.7	87.9	89.5	93.9
2 dwellings	11.6	15.6	11.0	9.2	5.0
3 and more	0.9	1.4	0.7	0.5	0.3
None	0.5	0.3	0.4	0.9	0.8
By structure					
Reinforced concrete structure	12.5	15.7	13.5	9.5	5.3
Brick and concrete structure	57.2	57.9	65.3	50.6	47.8
Brick (stone) wood structure	26.0	25.1	18.9	30.9	42.5
Bamboo-grass adobe structure	2.8	0.9	1.5	5.9	3.6
Others	1.4	0.5	0.8	3.1	0.9
Number of families owning commercial residential flats	1997	767	557	577	96
Rural households owning commercial residential flats (as percentage of total families owning commercial residential flats)	8.7	10.1	8.1	8.0	7.4

II. Drinking Water

109.95 million rural households drank purified tap water, accounting for 47.7%; 95.72 million drank protected well water or spring water, accounting for 41.6%; 20.11 million drank unprotected well water or spring water, accounting for 8.7%; 1.3 million drank river and lake water, accounting for 0.6%; 1.55 million drank collected rainfall water, accounting for 0.7%; 670,000 drank barreled water, accounting for 0.3%; and 960,000 households drank water from other sources, accounting for 0.4%.

Table 2 Household Composition by Drinking Water Source

Unit: %

Items	Nationwide	East China	Central China	West China	Northeast China
Purified tap water	47. 7	62. 3	43. 9	38. 2	36. 1
Water from protected wells or springs	41. 6	33. 5	42. 8	45. 8	58. 5
Water from unprotected wells or springs	8. 7	3. 5	11. 9	11. 8	5. 3
Water from rivers and lakes	0. 6	0. 1	0. 4	1. 3	0. 0
Collected rainfall water	0. 7	0. 0	0. 4	1. 7	0. 0
Barreled water	0. 3	0. 2	0. 4	0. 4	0. 0
Other water sources	0. 4	0. 3	0. 3	0. 8	0. 1

III. Sanitation Facilities

83. 39 million rural households used water-flush sanitary toilets, accounting for 36. 2%; 7. 21 million used water-flash non-sanitary toilets, accounting for 3. 1%; 28. 59 million used hygienic pit toilets, accounting for 12. 4%; 106. 39 million used ordinary pit toilets, accounting for 46. 2%; there were 4. 69 million rural households without toilets, accounting for 2. 0%.

Table 3 Household Composition by Home Sanitation Facilities

Unit: %

Items	Nationwide	East China	Central China	West China	Northeast China
Water-flush sanitary toilet	36. 2	54. 2	29. 2	29. 7	4. 1
Water-flush non-sanitary toilet	3. 1	2. 1	4. 1	3. 8	0. 2
Hygienic pit toilet	12. 4	11. 7	13. 6	12. 0	12. 2
Ordinary pit toilet	46. 2	30. 8	52. 2	50. 1	82. 9
Rural households without toilet	2. 0	1. 2	0. 9	4. 3	0. 5

IV. Possession of Durable Consumer Goods

Every 100 rural households possessed 24. 8 cars, 101. 9 motorcycles and electromobiles, 57. 2 water heaters for showering, 52. 8 air-conditioners, 85. 9 refrigerators, 115. 2 color TVs, 32. 2 computers and 244. 3 cellphones.

Table 4 Possession of Durable Consumer Goods

Items	Unit	Nationwide	East China	Central China	West China	Northeast China
Cars	Per 100 rural households	24.8	33.7	22.4	18.8	17.6
Motorcycles and electrombiles	Per 100 rural households	101.9	131.9	106.6	72.9	63.0
Waterheaters for showering	Per 100 rural households	57.2	77.2	59.4	42.5	10.3
Air-conditioners	Per 100 rural households	52.8	86.8	58.5	20.5	2.2
Refrigerators	Per 100 rural households	85.9	94.9	87.1	75.1	86.2
Color TV	Per 100 rural households	115.2	128.6	115.3	102.6	106.6
Percentage of household accounted by method for receiving TV program						
#Cable TV	%	57.3	76.1	53.1	36.2	83.2
Satellite TV	%	40.5	20.5	44.8	62.7	15.1
Computers	Per 100 rural households	32.2	50.3	31.1	15.9	23.5
Cellphones	Per 100 rural households	244.3	247.9	247.4	243.1	214.0
Percentage of cellphones having access to the Internet	%	47.8	48.8	47.4	47.4	46.2

Note: The household percentage by receiving mode for TV programs is the ratio of rural households with certain modes of TV program access to the number of households with color televisions. The percentage of cellphones having access to the Internet is the ratio of cellphones having access to the Internet to the total number of cellphones owned by the enumerated households.

V. Primary Residential Energy Resources

135.03 million rural households mainly used electricity for cooking and heating, accounting for 58.6%; 113.47 million mainly used coal gas, natural gas and liquefied petroleum gas, accounting for 49.3%; 101.77 million mainly used firewood, accounting for 44.2%; 55.06 million mainly used coal, accounting for 23.9%; 1.56 million mainly used biogas, accounting for 0.7%; 1.26 million mainly used other energy resources, accounting for 0.5%; and 560,000 mainly used solar energy, accounting for 0.2%.

Table 5 Composition of Primary Residential Energy Resource

Unit: %

Items	Nationwide	East China	Central China	West China	Northeast China
Firewood	44.2	27.4	40.1	58.6	84.5
Coal	23.9	29.4	16.3	24.8	27.4
Coal gas, natural gas and liquefied petroleum gas	49.3	69.5	58.2	24.5	20.3
Biogas	0.7	0.3	0.7	1.2	0.1
Electricity	58.6	57.2	59.3	59.5	58.7
Solar energy	0.2	0.2	0.3	0.3	0.1
Others	0.5	0.2	0.2	1.3	0.1

Note: Each household can choose two options for this indicator and therefore the aggregate value of all options exceeds 100%.

Notes:

1. Dwelling: a building for human habitation, with such structures as wall, roof, door, and window, and the surrounded walls can protect people from rain and wind. According to the living habits of different locality, caves, bamboo huts, yurts, tents, yurt and houseboats are also included.

2. Energy for cooking and heating: energy used for cooking and heating by the household, including firewood, coal, gas, natural gas, liquefied petroleum gas, biogas, electricity, solar energy, and other energy such as cow dung.

3. Four major regions: East China includes Beijing Municipality, Tianjin Municipality, Hebei Province, Shanghai Municipality, Jiangsu Province, Zhejiang Province, Fujian Province, Shandong Province, Guangdong Province and Hainan Province. Central China includes Shanxi Province, Anhui Province, Jiangxi Province, Henan Province, Hubei Province and Hunan Province. West China includes Inner Mongolia Autonomous Region, Guangxi Zhuang Autonomous Region, Chongqing Municipality, Sichuan Province, Guizhou Province, Yunnan Province, Tibet Autonomous Region, Shaanxi Province, Gansu Province, Qinghai Province, Ningxia Hui Autonomous Region and Xinjiang Uygur Autonomous Region. Northeast China includes Liaoning Province, Jilin Province and Heilongjiang Province.

4. Because of rounding after the decimal point, sums of individual items may not equal to the total.

Communique of the Third National Agricultural Census (No. 5)

Agriculture Operators

The Steering Group Office of the Third National Agricultural Census of the State Council
National Bureau of Statistics of China
December 16, 2017

The Third National Agricultural Census investigated the agriculture operators. The following are the results of the enumeration:

I. Number and Structure of the Agriculture Operators

In 2016, the number of agriculture operators was 314.22 million, including 149.27 million females. Among them, 60.23 million were aged 35 and below; 148.48 million were between the ages of 36 and 54; 105.51 million were aged 55 and above.

Table 1 Number and Structure of the Agriculture Operators

Unit: × 10,000, %

Items	Nationwide	East China	Central China	West China	Northeast China
Total number of agriculture operators	31422	8746	9809	10734	2133
Structure of agriculture operators by sex					
Male	52. 5	52. 4	52. 6	52. 1	54. 3
Female	47. 5	47. 6	47. 4	47. 9	45. 7
Structure of agriculture operators by age					
35 and below	19. 2	17. 6	18. 0	21. 9	17. 6
36—54	47. 3	44. 5	47. 7	48. 6	49. 8
55 and above	33. 6	37. 9	34. 4	29. 5	32. 6
Structure of agriculture operators by educational degree					
Illiterate	6. 4	5. 3	5. 7	8. 7	1. 9
Primary school	37. 0	32. 5	32. 7	44. 7	36. 1
Junior high school	48. 4	52. 5	52. 6	39. 9	55. 0
Senior high or technical secondary school	7. 1	8. 5	7. 9	5. 4	5. 6
Vocational school and above	1. 2	1. 2	1. 1	1. 2	1. 4
Structure of agriculture operators by subsector					
Crop Farming	92. 9	93. 3	94. 4	91. 8	90. 1
Forestry	2. 2	2. 0	1. 8	2. 8	2. 0
Livestock	3. 5	2. 4	2. 6	4. 6	6. 4
Aquaculture and fisheries	0. 8	1. 6	0. 6	0. 3	0. 5
Services for agriculture	0. 6	0. 7	0. 6	0. 5	1. 0

II. Number and Structure of the Agriculture Operators from Large-scale Agricultural Households

In 2016, there were 12. 89 million agriculture operators from large-scale agricultural households (including engaged household members and employees), including 6. 09 million females, 2. 72 million aged 35 and below, 7. 51 million aged between 36 and 54, 2. 66 million aged 55 and above.

Table 2 Number and Structure of the Agriculture Operators from Large-scale Agricultural Households

Unit: ×10,000 , %

Items	Nationwide	East China	Central China	West China	Northeast China
Total number of agriculture operators	1289	382	280	411	217
Structure of agriculture operators by sex					
Male	52. 8	54. 0	53. 7	50. 0	54. 7
Female	47. 2	46. 0	46. 3	50. 0	45. 3
Structure of agriculture operators by age					
35 and below	21. 1	16. 8	17. 1	27. 0	22. 6
36—54	58. 3	57. 8	58. 7	57. 9	59. 2
55 and above	20. 7	25. 4	24. 3	15. 1	18. 2
Structure of agriculture operators by educational degree					
Illiterate	3. 6	3. 4	3. 7	5. 2	1. 0
Primary school	30. 6	28. 8	26. 9	35. 7	28. 6
Junior high school	55. 4	56. 5	56. 8	48. 6	64. 3
Senior high or technical secondary school	8. 9	9. 9	11. 2	8. 4	5. 2
Vocational school and above	1. 5	1. 3	1. 4	2. 1	0. 9
Structure of agriculture operators by subsector					
Crop Farming	67. 7	60. 0	60. 9	73. 3	79. 8
Forestry	2. 7	2. 9	3. 0	3. 1	1. 1
Livestock	21. 3	19. 3	28. 6	21. 6	14. 6
Aquaculture and fisheries	6. 4	15. 5	4. 6	1. 0	2. 8
Services for agriculture	1. 9	2. 3	2. 9	1. 1	1. 6

III. Number and Structure of the Agriculture Operators from Agricultural Enterprises

In 2016, there were 10. 92 million agriculture operators from agricultural enterprises, including 4. 44 million females, 2. 15 million aged 35 and below, 6. 68 million aged between 36 and 54, and 2. 09 million aged 55 and above.

Table 3 Number and Structure of the Agriculture Operators from Agricultural Enterprises

Unit: ×10,000 , %

Items	Nationwide	East China	Central China	West China	Northeast China
Total number of agriculture operators	1092	341	265	358	128
Structure of agriculture operators by sex					
Male	59.4	59.1	60.1	56.7	66.1
Female	40.6	40.9	39.9	43.3	33.9
Structure of agriculture operators by age					
35 and below	19.7	17.0	17.1	23.1	22.9
36—54	61.2	59.7	61.2	61.7	63.6
55 and above	19.1	23.3	21.7	15.3	13.5
Structure of agriculture operators by educational degree					
Illiterate	3.5	3.4	3.5	4.6	1.2
Primary school	21.8	23.4	20.6	25.6	9.8
Junior high school	47.0	48.6	49.7	44.3	44.5
Senior high or technical secondary school	19.6	17.9	20.1	16.7	31.3
Vocational school and above	8.0	6.7	6.1	8.9	13.2
Structure of agriculture operators by subsector					
Crop Farming	50.3	49.6	49.1	50.7	53.3
Forestry	16.4	14.9	14.9	16.7	22.6
Livestock	16.6	14.7	18.7	18.6	11.8
Aquaculture and fisheries	6.2	10.5	5.8	3.4	2.9
Services for agriculture	10.6	10.4	11.5	10.6	9.5

Notes:

1. Agriculture Operators: the number of persons (including persons employed on a part-time basis) of agricultural households or agricultural enterprises who have been engaged in agricultural production and service activities for more than 30 days.

2. Four regions: East China includes Beijing Municipality, Tianjin Municipality, Hebei Province, Shanghai Municipality, Jiangsu Province, Zhejiang Province, Fujian Province, Shandong Province, Guangdong Province and Hainan Province. Central China includes Shanxi Province, Anhui Province, Jiangxi Province, Henan Province, Hubei Province and Hunan Province. West China includes Inner Mongolia Autonomous Region, Guangxi Zhuang Autonomous Region, Chongqing Municipality, Sichuan Province, Guizhou Province, Yunnan Province, Tibet Autonomous Region, Shaanxi Province, Gansu Province, Qinghai Province, Ningxia Hui Autonomous Region and Xinjiang Uygur Autonomous Region. Northeast China includes Liaoning Province, Jilin Province and Heilongjiang Province.

3. Because of rounding after the decimal point, sums of individual items may not equal to the total.

The Development of Agriculture, Rural Areas and Farmers in China Attracts Worldwide Attention and Chinese Rural Revitalization Remains a Long-term and Arduous Task

- The Results of the Third National Agricultural Census Indicate Historic Changes in the Development of Agriculture, Rural Areas and Farmers

Deputy Chief of the Steering Group Office of the Third National Agricultural Census of the State Council
Commissioner of the National Bureau of Statistics of China
Ning Jizhe

The Report of the 19th National Congress of the Communist Party of China (CPC), pointed out that addressing the issues of agriculture, rural areas and farmers shall be the top priority of the Party's work, the rural revitalization strategy shall be implemented, which provides guidance for the development of agriculture, rural areas and farmers in the new era. The Third National Agricultural Census that lasted for more than three years has been successfully completed in China as an effort to deepen the study and implementation of the spirits of the 19th CPC National Congress. The results of the Census provided important statistical support for comprehensive and accurate understanding of the basic national conditions related to the issues of agriculture, rural areas and farmers and the implementation of the rural revitalization strategy. The results of the Third National Agricultural Census showed that, since the 18th CPC National Congress, under the guidance of Xi Jinping's Thought on Socialism with Chinese Characteristics for a New Era and the sound leadership of the CPC Central Committee and the State Council, the system of agricultural support and protection has been constantly optimized, the policy support to boost agriculture, benefit farmers and increase rural prosperity has been constantly increased; with remarkable progress in modernization of agriculture, rural environment and farmers' living condition have been noticeably improved, laying a solid foundation for building a moderately prosperous society in all respects and implementing the rural revitalization strategy.

I. Remarkable progress in modernization of agriculture

The prosperity of the industry is the foundation for rural revitalization. General Secretary Xi Jinping has reiterated that agriculture is a vital industry in China. In recent years, especially since the 18th CPC National Congress, the CPC Central Committee and the State Council have attached great importance to the issues of agriculture, rural areas and farmers, adopted a series of policies and measures to continuously increase their support for agriculture, improve agricultural infrastructure and equipment, and consolidate the agricultural foundation to ensure the national food security and the basic supply of bulk agricultural products; focused on agricultural supply-side structural reforms, optimized the structure of agricultural products, increased efficiency and competitiveness of China's agriculture industry; constantly deepened rural reforms by adhering to the principle of the separating rural land ownership rights, contract rights and management rights, promoted the land ownership certification system, improved the system of land ownership, fostered new types of agricultural business entities, increased the vitality of the agriculture industry, and provided a strong institutional support; transferred the agricultural growth mode and advanced the modernization of agriculture.

1. The overall agricultural productivity was remarkably enhanced. Feeding more than 1.3 billion Chinese people has always been the top priority of the Chinese government. General Secretary Xi Jinping repeatedly stressed that "we must be the main provider of our own food". In recent years, China's overall agricultural productivity has witnessed noticeable in-

crease and its ability to ensure national food security and the basic supply of bulk agricultural products has been improved significantly. The total grain production in 2006 was below 1 trillion jin in 2006. In 2013 China's total grain production exceeded 1. 2 trillion jin for the first time. The number remained at a level above 1. 2 trillion jin from 2014-2017. The new level of overall grain productivity ensures national food security. The total production of meat and aquatic products ranked first in the world. The production of main cash crops such as cotton, oilseeds, sugar crops, vegetable and fruit remained high, laying a solid foundation for the supply of bulk agricultural products to meet basic needs.

2. Irrigation conditions were significantly improved. Optimized agricultural infrastructure is not only the basic guarantee to improving overall agricultural productivity but also an important symbol of modern agriculture. The results of the Third National Agricultural Census showed that the conditions of irrigation and water conservation in China have been significantly improved and China's ability to resist natural disasters has been strengthened. As of the end of 2016, the number of electromechanical wells and irrigation and drainage stations that can be used normally in China increased by 8. 2% and 8. 9% respectively as compared to that at the end of 2006, the number of irrigable reservoirs and reservoirs that can be used normally increased by 53. 3%. In 2016, irrigated arable land accounted for 55. 2% of the actual arable land, which laid a solid foundation for agricultural production.

3. Agricultural mechanization reached a high level. The rapid growth and widespread application of agricultural machinery has not only greatly increased labor productivity, but also gradually liberated farmers from labor-intensive farming. The results of the Third National Agricultural Census showed that by the end of 2016, the number of combine harvesters and threshers in China was 1. 14 million, up 105. 3% over the end of 2006, 14. 31 million irrigation and drainage machines, up 6. 1% over the end of 2006. The farming of the three major grain crops achieved a high level of mechanization. The proportions of mechanized tillage, sowing and harvesting of wheat reached 94. 5%, 82. 0% and 92. 2%, respectively. The proportions of mechanized tillage, sowing and harvesting of maize were 73. 7%, 69. 9% and 61. 7%, respectively. The proportions of mechanized tillage, sowing and harvesting of rice were 83. 3%, 29. 0% and 80. 1%, respectively.

4. Facility agriculture were developed quickly. The number of plastic nurseries, greenhouses and other agricultural facilities grew rapidly, changing the spatial and temporal distri-

bution of agricultural production to meet the people's growing diversified needs. The results of the Third National Agricultural Census showed that by the end of 2016, the aggregate area of greenhouses in China reached 334,000 hectares, up 312.6% over the end of 2006, the area covered by plastic nurseries was 981,000 hectares, up 111.0% over the end of 2006. The total area of greenhouses and plastic nurseries in China ranked the first in the world. China also experiencing a fast-agricultural industrialization process.

5. The overall quality of agriculture operators was improved significantly. China saw an accelerated transfer of rural labor force to other sectors and a steady progress in citizenization, the number of agriculture operators dropped. According to the results of the Third National Agricultural Census, the number of agriculture operators activities in China for more than a month in 2016 was 314 million, down 8.7% compared to that of 2006. The overall literacy quality of agriculture operators improved significantly. In 2016, the percentage of agriculture operators with junior high school education reached 48.4%, up 3.3 percentage points over 2006; senior high school or technical secondary school education 7.1%, up 3.0 percentage points over 2006; and vocational school education and above 1.2%, up 1.0 percentage points over 2006.

6. A large number of new agricultural production and operation entities emerged. New agricultural production and operation entities are the leading force in the modernization of agriculture. In recent years, China has increased its support for new agricultural production and operation entities in areas such as infrastructure development, industry and commerce, public finance, taxation, finance and insurance and land use. Farmer cooperatives, household-based farms, agricultural enterprises and many other types of agricultural entities have emerged. The results of the Third National Agricultural Census showed that by the end of 2016, the number of agricultural entities in China was 2.04 million, up 417.4% over the end of 2006. Farmer cooperatives have grown from nothing and developed rapidly, the organizational level of agricultural production and operation was increased. As of the end of 2016, there were 910,000 farmer cooperatives engaged in agricultural production or operation.

7. Large-scale farming have developed rapidly. According to the results of the Third National Agricultural Census, the proportion of arable land under large-scale operation to total arable land area in 2016 was 28.6%. Among the arable land under large-scale operation, those managed by large household-based agricultural operators accounted for 17.0% and those man-

aged by agricultural enterprises accounted for 11. 6%. The number of inventory of pigs raised by large-scale holdings accounted for 62. 9% of the total pig inventory in China and the number of poultry raised by large-scale holdings accounted for 73. 9% of the total inventory of poultry in China. The rapid development of large-scale holdings plays an important and positive role in stabilizing agricultural production, the supply of agricultural products and the agricultural markets.

II. The environment in rural areas was noticeably improved

If China wants to be beautiful, the countryside must be beautiful. In recent years, thanks to government support, rural infrastructure (water supply, power supply, etc.) and rural environment in China have been improved significantly.

1. The number of township and village governance organizations decreased. As the urbanization process accelerated, the number of township and village governance organizations has decreased. The results of the Third National Agricultural Census showed that China had 31,925 townships and towns at the end of 2016, down 8. 1% compared to 2006; 596,450 village committees and agriculture-related neighborhood committees, down 6. 4% compared to 2006; 3. 17 million natural villages, down 3. 8% compared to 2006.

2. Rural infrastructure improved significantly. The central government has developed plans for the coordinated development of urban and rural areas, aiming to improve rural infrastructure. The results of the Third National Agricultural Census showed that, by the end of 2016, villages having access to the nationwide highway network accounted for 99. 3% of the total villages in China, up 3. 8 percentage points over 2006; villages having access to cement roads linked to main road network accounted for 76. 4% of the total villages, up 41. 2 percentage points; villages with cement roads within its boundaries as their main roads accounted for 80. 9% of the total villages, up 53. 2 percentage points; and villages with main roads having street lamps accounted for 61. 9%, up 40. 1 percentage points. The percentage of villages having access to electricity was 99. 7%, up 1 percentage point over 2006; villages with landline services 99. 5%, up 1. 9 percentage points; villages with cable TV 82. 8%, up 25. 4 percentage points; villages with broadband services were approximately 90%. There were 73. 9% of villages had access to centralized or partially centralized garbage management services, up 58. 1 percentage points.

3. Access to fundamental public services in rural areas improved. As of the end of 2016, villages with kindergartens and nurseries accounted for 32.3% of all villages in China, up 2.2 percentage points over 2006; villages with fitness facilities accounted for 59.2% of all villages in China, up 48.5 percentage points; villages with recreational facilities accounted for 41.3%, up 26.2 percentage points; and villages with health care facilities accounted for 81.9%, up 7.6 percentage points.

4. New industries and business modes in rural areas developed rapidly. As of the end of 2016, villages engaged in tourism accounted for 4.9% of all villages in China, up 2.7 percentage points over 2006; and e-commerce is starting from scratch in China's rural areas. In 2016, more than one-fourth of the villages in China had e-commerce distribution sites. There were 44,000 large-scale rural households and 51,000 agricultural enterprises selling agricultural products through e-commerce. There were 486,000 rural households and 131,000 agricultural enterprises engaged in operation of facility agriculture; 126,000 large-scale rural households and 72,000 agricultural enterprises engaged in circular agricultural production; and 18,000 rural households and 25,000 agricultural enterprises engaged in industrialized agricultural production. Many startups operated by rural returnees from urban areas have added new vitality to rural development.

III. The living standard of farmers was obviously improved

To help farmers get rich is a crucial part of China's effort to build a moderately prosperous society. The report of the 19th National Congress of the CPC emphasized that the aspirations of the people to live a better life must always be the focus of the CPC's efforts and improving the well-being of people is the fundamental goal of development. In recent years, especially since the 18th CPC National Congress, the central government has taken many measures to tap the internal revenue-generating potentials of agriculture and increase farmers' sources of income. Thanks to these efforts, farmers' income and sense of gain and happiness have increased rapidly and their life quality has improved significantly.

1. Farmers' income continued to grow rapidly. According to the results of urban and rural household survey, the per capita disposable income of rural residents in 2016 reached 12,363 RMB, up 47.4% over 2012 with a real increase of 36.3% and an average annual growth rate of 8.0%. Since the 18th National Congress of the CPC, the average annual growth rate of per

capita disposable income of rural residents has been 1.5 percentage points higher than that of urban residents, and the widening gap between urban and rural residents' income growth has been successfully reversed. In 2016, the ratio of per capita disposable income of urban resident to that of rural residents was 2.72 (provided that per capita disposal income of rural residents was 1), down 0.16 over 2012. The Engel coefficient of rural residents was 32.2%, down 5.3 percentage points over 2012, and the living standard of farmers continued to improve.

2. The housing conditions of farmers improved. According to the results of the Third National Agricultural Census, 99.5% of rural households possessed their own dwellings by the end of 2016, up 0.2 percentage points over 2006. Among them, rural households with one dwelling accounted for 87.0%, down 5.5 percentage points over 2006; rural households with two and three dwellings accounted for 11.6% and 0.9% respectively, up 5.2 percentage points and 0.5 percentage points respectively. The number of rural households owning commercial apartments reached 19.97 million, accounting for 8.7% of the total number of rural households, whereas few households purchased commercial apartments a decade ago. Houses with brick-concrete structures accounted for 57.2% of the total houses owned by rural households, up 17.8 percentage points over 2006; houses with reinforced concrete structures accounted for 12.5%, up 6.5 percentage points; houses with brick and stone structure and bamboo, grass and adobe structure accounted for 26.0% and 2.8%, down 18.3 percentage points and 6.8 percentage points respectively.

3. Drinking water became safer. Because of rural drinking water safety projects, the safety of drinking water in rural areas has significantly increased. According to the results of the Third National Agricultural Census, in 2016, nearly 110 million rural households in China drank purified tap water, accounting for 47.7% of all rural households, up 24.6 percentage points over 2006.

4. More farmers used cleaner energy for cooking and heating. With the gradual improvement of rural infrastructure conditions, the energy structure in rural areas has undergone major changes. The primary energy used for cooking and heating has been changed from firewood and coal to cleaner energy such as electricity, natural gas and liquefied petroleum gas. More farmers have adopted a greener life style. In 2016, 135.03 million rural households used electricity for cooking and heating[①], accounting for 58.6% of the total rural households in China,

① Each household could choose two options for this indicator and therefore the aggregate value of all proportions exceeds 100%.

up 57. 8 percentage points over 2006; 113. 47 million households mainly used gas, natural gas and liquefied petroleum gas for cooking and heating, accounting for 49. 3% of the total rural households, up 37. 4 percentage points.

5. Sanitary facilities improved. In 2016, there were 83. 39 million rural households using flush toilets, accounting for 36. 2% of the total rural households, and 28. 59 million households using pit toilet, accounting for 12. 4% of the total rural households.

6. The possession of durable consumer goods increased. In 2016, the average car ownership per 100 rural households in China was 24. 8, up 21. 4 over 2006; color TV 115. 2, up 27. 9; computers 32. 2, up 30. 0; mobile phones 244. 3, up 174. 5.

Since the 18th National Congress of the CPC, thanks to the joint efforts of all regions and all government departments under the guidance of Xi Jinping's Thought on Socialism with Chinese Characteristics for a New Era and the sound leadership of the CPC Central Committee and the State Council, historic changes have taken place in agriculture, rural areas and farmers; remarkable progress has been made in the modernization of agriculture; and rural environment and the living standard of farmers have been noticeably improved. However, we must clearly recognized that agricultural modernization is still insufficient for integrating the development of industrialization, information technology, urbanization and agricultural modernization and that rural areas are holding back China's effort to build a moderately prosperous society in all respects. The unbalanced and insufficient development between rural and urban areas of China remains one of our most prominent problems. We shall rally closely around the CPC Central Committee with Xi Jinping at the core, take Xi Jinping's Thought on Socialism with Chinese Characteristics for a New Era as the overarching principle, put into practice of the new development philosophy, implement the rural revitalization strategy, properly resolve relevant risks and challenges, secure a decisive victory in building a moderately prosperous society in all respects and strive for the great success of socialism with Chinese characteristics for a new era.

一图看懂农普公报：

十年来，农村的变化这么大！

国家统计局日前发布的第三次全国农业普查结果显示，十年来尤其是党的十八大以来，在习近平新时代中国特色社会主义思想指导下，在党中央、国务院坚强正确领导下，在各地区各部门共同努力下，“三农”发生历史性变革，现代农业建设成就辉煌，农村面貌和环境水平明显改善，农民生活质量和水平显著提高，为世界所瞩目。

一、农业生产经营人员素质更高

农业生产经营人员受教育程度（单位 %）

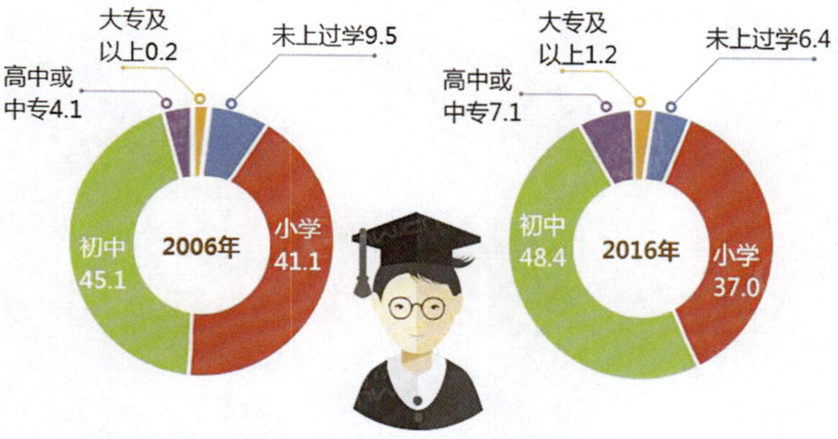

2016年农业生产经营人员数量3.14亿人，比2006年下降8.7%，但素质更高，拥有高中或中专文化的比重比2006年提升3.0个百分点；大专及以上文化提升1.0个百分点。

二、农田水利设施明显改善

灌溉耕地面积超五成

三、农业机械化水平快速提高

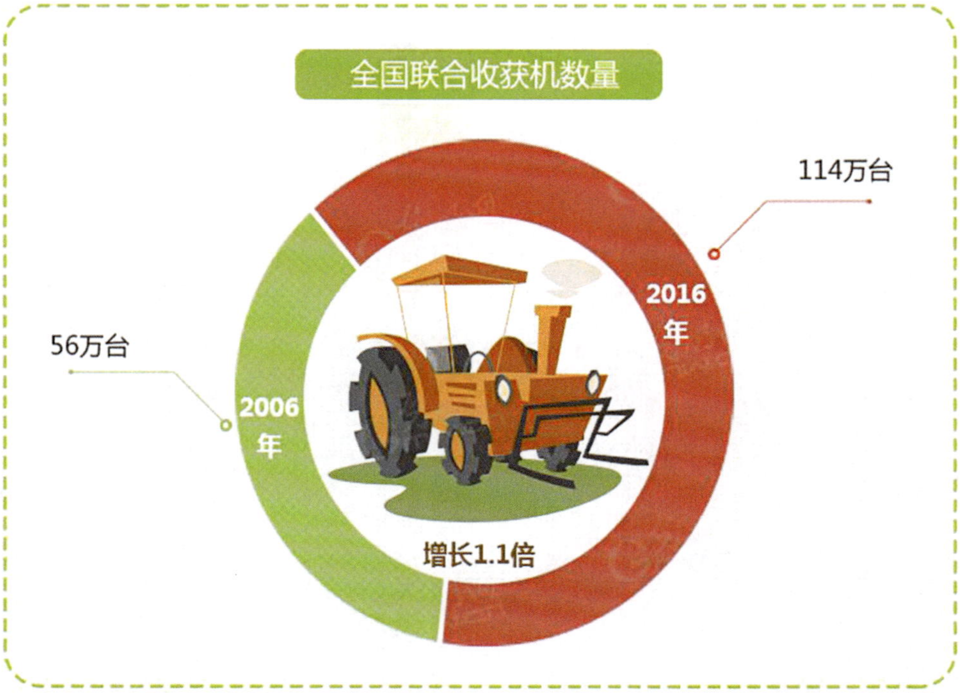

四、设施农业较快发展

全国温室和大棚占地面积

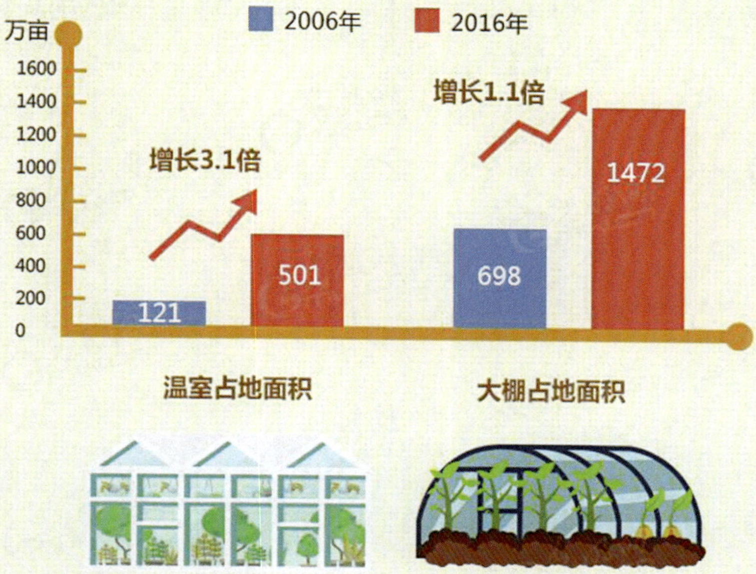

五、规模经营发展迅速

2016年耕地、生猪、家禽规模化水平 （单位%）

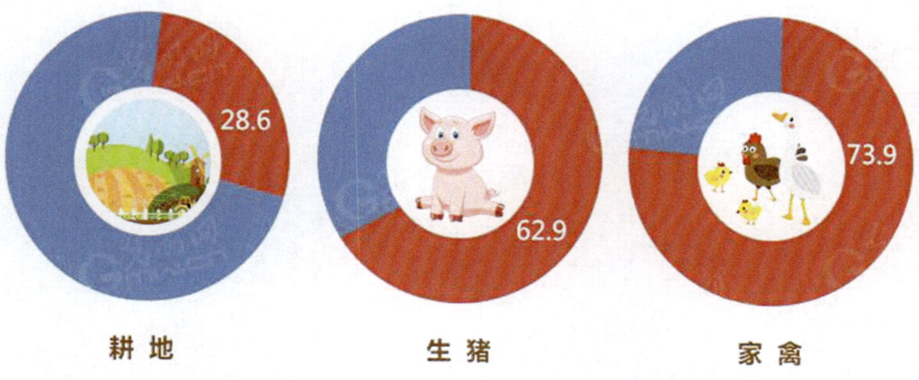

2016年耕地规模化耕种面积占比28.6%，规模生猪存栏占比62.9%，规模家禽存栏占比73.9%。

六、农村交通更便利

村通公路和村内道路照明

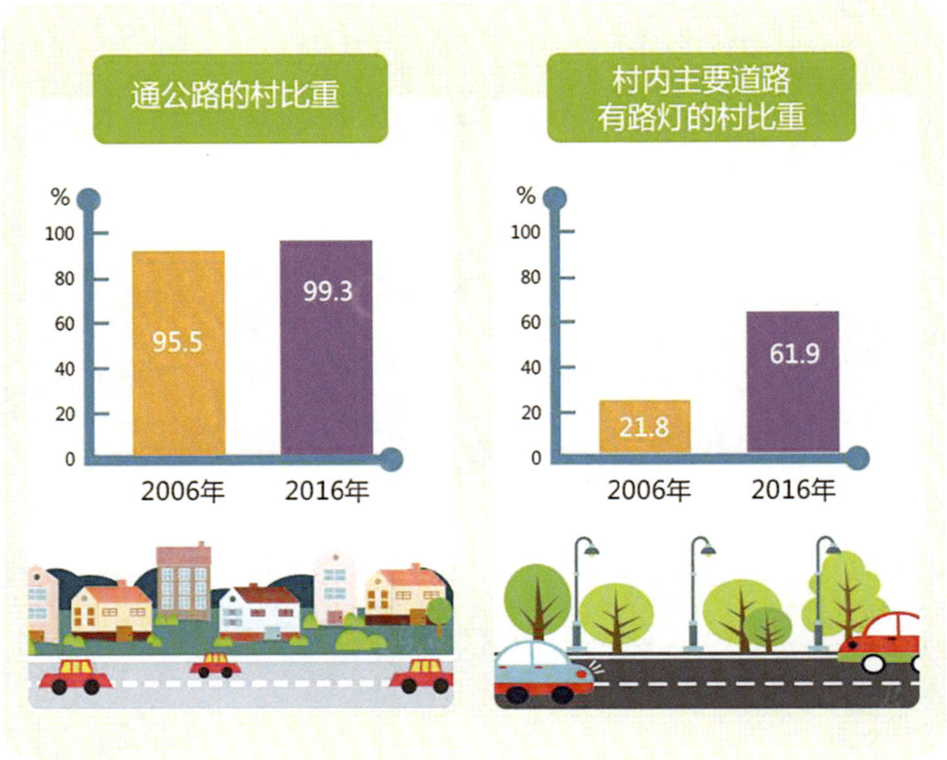

七、通电、通电话和安装有线电视的村比重提高

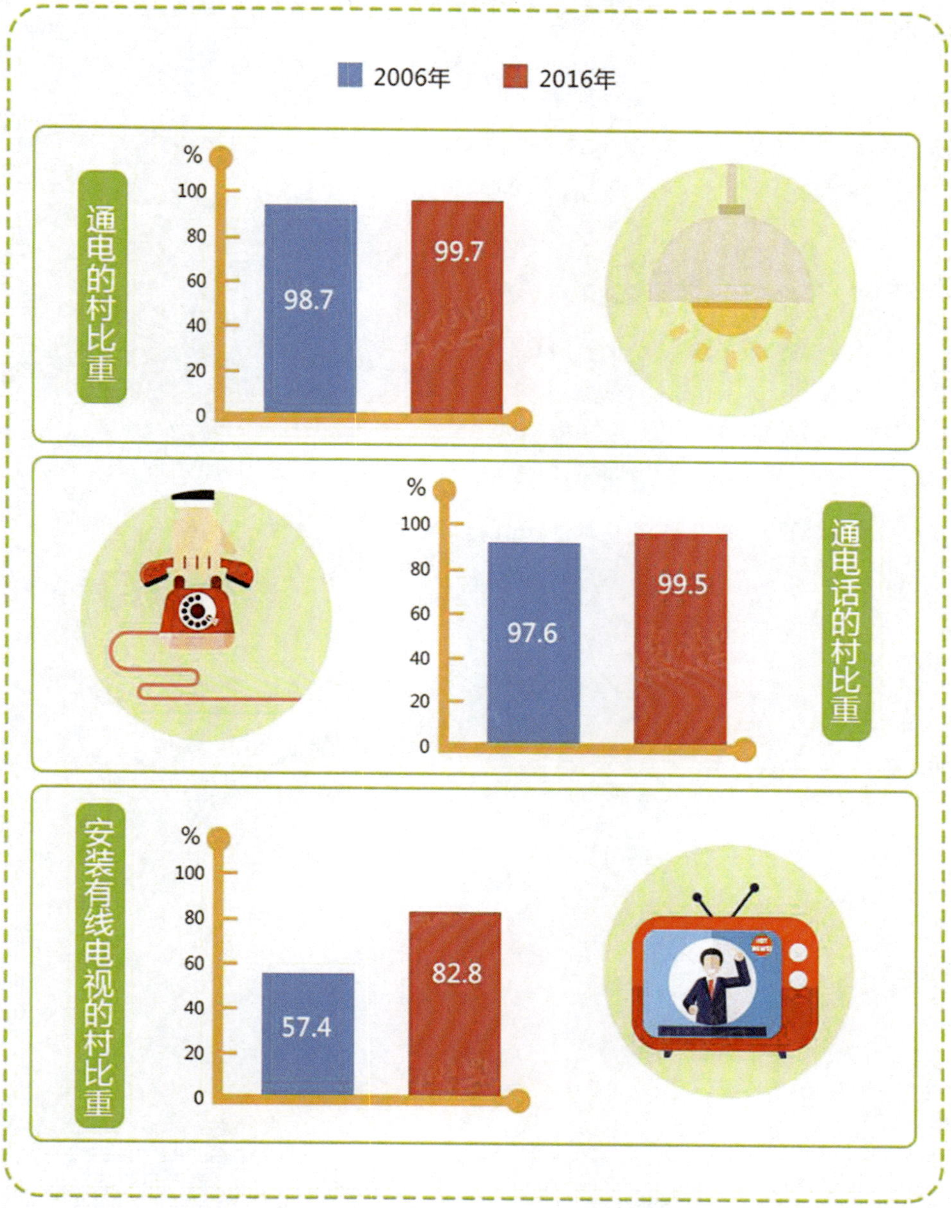

八、基本公共服务覆盖更广

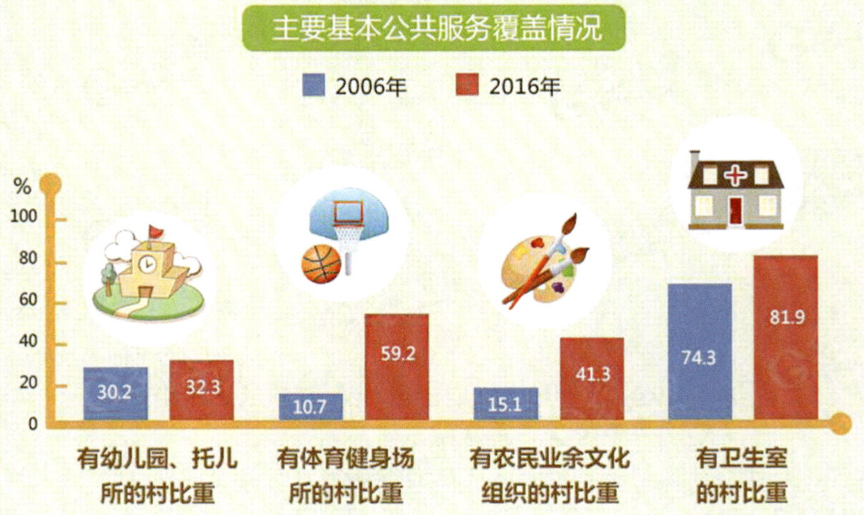

近1/3的村有幼儿园、托儿所；近6成有体育健身场所；超8成的村有卫生室。

九、农村环境显著改善

十、农民住房质量提高

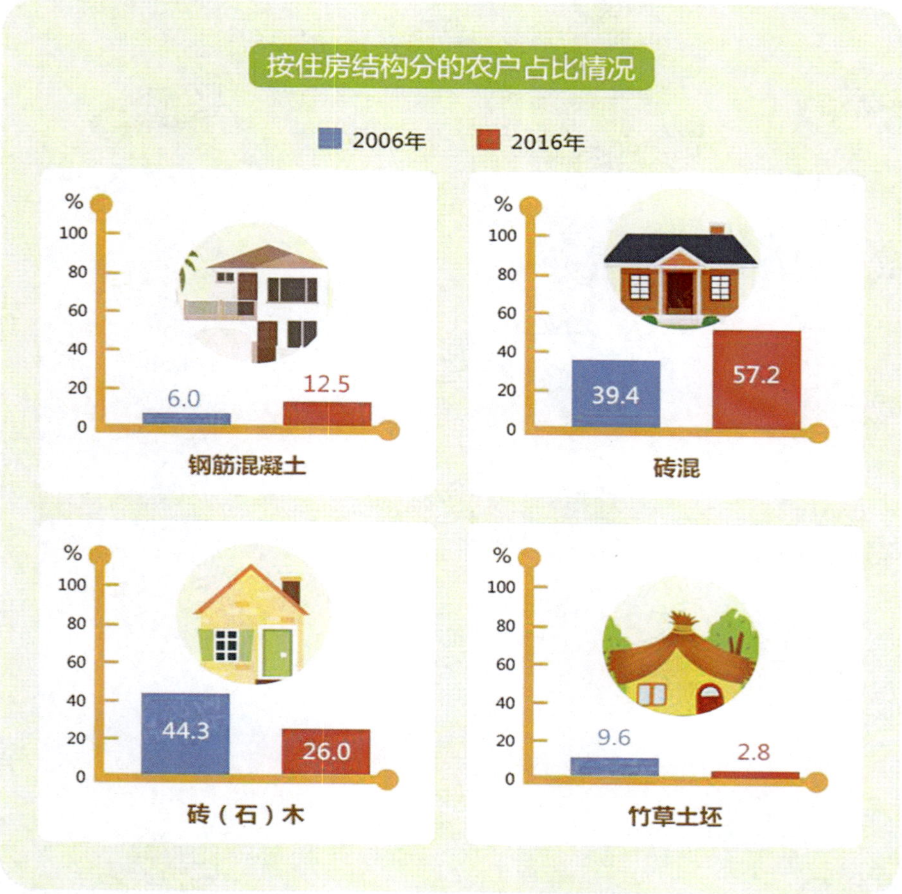

十一、农民饮水更安全

接近一半农户饮用经过集中净化处理的自来水

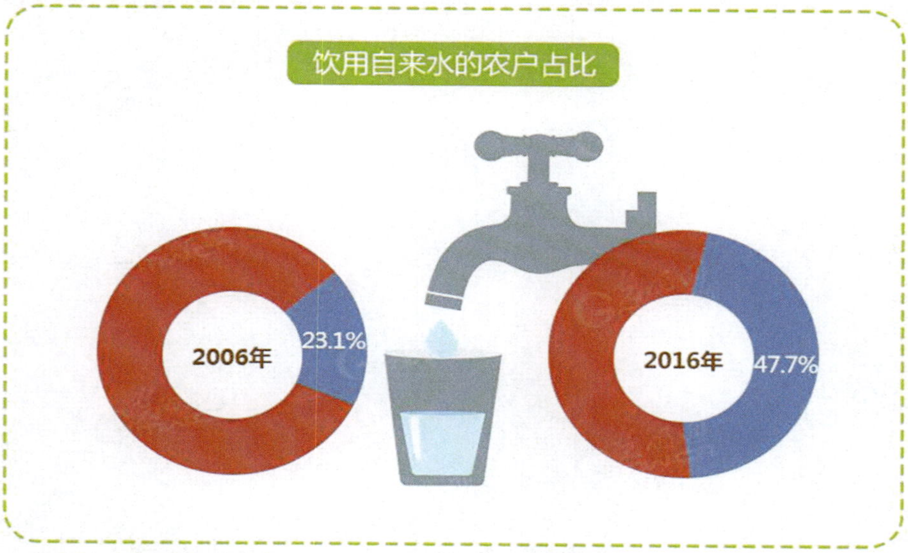

十二、农户耐用消费品拥有量快速增加

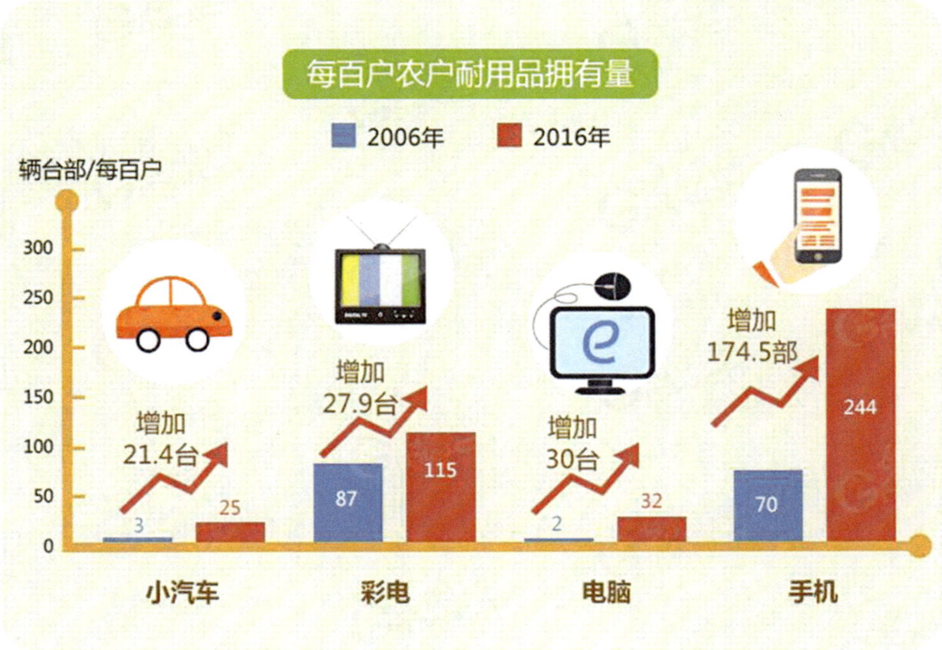

出 品：国务院第三次全国农业普查领导小组办公室 ；光明网【改革光明论】栏目

资料来源：国家统计局　编 辑：张 琳　设 计：耿楠楠